ALSO BY ALEXANDRA PETRI

NOTHING IS WRONG AND
HERE IS WHY

A FIELD GUIDE TO AWKWARD SILENCES

ALEXANDRA PETRI'S US HISTORY

Important American Documents
(I Made Up)

ALEXANDRA PETRI

W. W. NORTON & COMPANY
Independent Publishers Since 1923

For information about permission to reproduce selections from
this book, write to Permissions, W. W. Norton & Company, Inc.,
500 Fifth Avenue, New York, NY 10110

For information about special discounts for bulk purchases,
please contact W. W. Norton Special Sales at
specialsales@wwnorton.com or 800-233-4830

Manufacturing by Lakeside Book Company
Book design by Lovedog Studio
Production manager: Lauren Abbate

Library of Congress Control Number: 2023951051

ISBN 978-1-324-07476-2 pbk.

W. W. Norton & Company, Inc.
500 Fifth Avenue, New York, N.Y. 10110
www.wwnorton.com

W. W. Norton & Company Ltd.
15 Carlisle Street, London W1D 3BS

1 2 3 4 5 6 7 8 9 0

ALEXANDRA PETRI'S
US HISTORY

For Emma,
whose prompt arrival ensured
that this manuscript's wasn't.
I hope you love to read.

Contents

Contents

Introduction

Some people look at our history textbooks and say, "Oh no! These books do not adequately express that all the Founders were perfect, radiant beings of pure light. We need a book that does that, and explains that America is the one place in the world where pulling yourself up by your bootstraps really works!" This is not that book.

Other people look at our history textbooks and say, "Yikes. American history is terrible in lots of ways we have not adequately reckoned with. We need a book that does a more accurate job of teaching about the whole past with all its failures and contradictions." I agree—but this is not that book either.

A third group of people look at our history textbooks and say, "Oh no! We have only one president's weird sex letters, and that president is Warren G. Harding! We need a book that fixes that!"

This is that book.

Hello! I'm Alexandra Petri. I write a humor column for *The Washington Post*. Am I a historian? Well, look. There is a famous saying that "history is written by the winners." So no, I'm not a historian, or a scholar, but now that I have written this book, I am something much more important: a winner.

And as a winner, I am here to address an urgent problem: our great national anger toward history. Sometimes it seems that being mad about the past is the only thing we can agree on. This anger toward history means that everyone is absolutely desperate to rewrite it. There seem to be two main ways of going about this. The first involves rewriting history to make it *more* accurate. This work is laudable but, like most laudable work, involves a high degree of difficulty and lots of painstaking research that requires you to sit in libraries for years and years and put your pens in a special locker and try not to spill coffee on important documents.

Then there is another way of rewriting history that doesn't require any research at all. But you do have to get yourself elected to some sort of state or federal office. Once there you can write a law that changes history to be anything you want, including what you only *wish* had happened.

But I wonder: If you're going to instruct all the educators in America to teach history that did not happen, why stop at saying slavery was actually not so bad or that Andrew Jackson was a swell guy? Why not actually commit to the principle of the thing and insert all the bizarre documents that you think ought to be there? Get weird with it! If you're going to lie about the past, lie big! And if anyone complains or asks questions, just start yelling about censorship and free speech. Or say you found it "in an archive." Most critics haven't been to any archives, and this bluff should silence them, I think.

So for anyone else who, like me, is interested in rewriting the American past badly and inaccurately, but in a fun way as opposed to a sinister way, what follows are some documents that, if I had my way, would have actually existed. I think when you read them, you will agree that these documents seem very authentic and that my writing them down for you was just a formality. Please don't use them in your actual history classes! Or do! Embrace the chaos!

If you are genuinely trying to study for the AP U.S. History exam and bought this book in error, I sincerely apologize.

ALEXANDRA PETRI'S
US HISTORY

★

Dear King Charles, I Have No Doubts About This Golden City and I Will Write You as Soon as I Am Back from It Bearing Tons of Gold

In the sixteenth century, a lot of people arrived in America from Europe with delusions of grandeur. These explorers and conquerors killed many people who were already living there and enslaved many more.

One such man was Francisco de Coronado. He was convinced that he was going to find seven cities of gold, which would be big money for Spain. Nothing would dissuade him. He embarked on a fruitless quest for this gold during which many people lost their lives, unfortunately not including Coronado himself. Along the way, he got kicked in the head by a horse, which sounds like it was extremely painful, although given what he did to the people he encountered, it is not hard to see the horse's point.

For years, scholars have looked for the last letter Coronado sent to Charles V, Holy Roman Emperor and King of Spain, before he set out on his ill-fated expedition for the golden city of Cibola. Well, the scholars can stop looking.

The Twentieth Day of April, Anno Domini 1541

Coronado here. Great news! There is gold in this land, much more gold than we even imagined! I have just heard a wonderful account from a captive whose name we have not bothered to learn, but for whom we have coined the nickname El Turco.* It is amazing how eager he is for us to follow him to find this treasure, especially considering that we put him in shackles, gave him this confusing nickname, and are on pretty hostile terms with the rest of his people. I guess he is just a stand-up guy.

We originally met him because we wanted someone to show us where to find more of the shaggy cows they have here, and he said, You don't want to find shaggy cows! You want to find something much, much better that just happens to be in the opposite direction!† That piqued our interest, especially when he remembered that what was in the other direction was a city of gold. At first he didn't remember how much gold was there, but then he started remembering more and more. This week he remembered that there was a whole tree covered in golden bells! This forgetfulness seems like it must be very inconvenient for him, but I'm always excited to hear about more gold.

The other captives are all downers; they insist that there "isn't any gold" and "he is trying to trick you and lead you into a trap." Which is just what they WOULD say, to trick us and keep their gold from us! They don't want us to know that they are fabulously wealthy, beyond our wildest imaginings, and have a leader who, as El Turco insists, "rides around on an enormous two-masted ship with a gold eagle at the front of it

---

* This is true.
† This is true.

that exactly matches the dimensions of a Spanish galleon, an image I came up with entirely on my own and did not cobble together using the suggestions of the men guarding me." Some people are suspicious that he is just telling us what we want to hear, but if that were true, why would he say that the city is full of golden eagles, golden dishware, and the love I was always denied by my father?

I think there's definitely gold. If there *weren't* any gold, would he keep using the word *acochis*, which we have decided to translate as "gold"? No, he wouldn't! But I don't see what else it could possibly mean. We showed him some other metal, and he said "That's not *acochis*!"* which shows how well he knows what gold truly is and how absolutely correct we are in our translation of that word. He even told us, "I swear, before I die, I shall see you have the *acochis* you deserve for what you have done!" The meaning is utterly unambiguous.

I should mention, though it probably isn't relevant, that we burned two hundred people on stakes right before his eyes. This is another reason I think we should leave soon; everyone else here has gotten weirdly hostile.

In case you were worried there was no tangible proof of this gold, don't worry. El Turco says that he used to "definitely" have a gold bracelet but "doesn't have it anymore."†

Some people say he isn't trustworthy because they saw him talking to the devil in a pitcher of water.‡ To me, that's a plus. I think the devil would know where gold is located!

He won't stop talking about the gold. The longer we stay

* This is true.
† This is true.
‡ This happened.

here among the Pueblo people, the more gold he remembers is due east across a very dangerous-looking river. As I was writing this, he just remembered that the king in Quivira eats exclusively off golden plates, and we've got to hurry there right now and grab them before he hears of our arrival. It's almost like he thinks it's urgent for us to leave, which wouldn't make any sense at all. I know for a fact that I am a great guest; all my friends in Spain were devastated when I left.

Anyway, we are almost ready to leave. Whenever we try to load our horses with supplies or bring food and other things we will need for the expedition, he says that it is not a good idea because we need to save more room for the gold and the horses will get overtired by carrying it.*

So wish us luck! All I can see in the direction we are going is forbidding territory where it might be easy to hide and ambush us, but I know there's no danger of that. Still, I am trying to load up with weapons, even though El Turco seems uneasy about it. Think of the gold, he says. You've got to leave room for the gold.

It's awesome how much he is looking out for us.

CWTFATG (Can't Wait to Find All That Gold),
Francisco de Coronado

---

* This happened.

Columbian Exchange Returns

"The Columbian Exchange" is the way we refer to the transfer of goods (and evils) that occurred from Europe to the Americas (and vice versa) after Christopher Columbus's expedition encountered the indigenous peoples of the Americas. Unfortunately, it did not work like most exchanges.

Thanks for patronizing the Columbian Exchange!

I'd like to return an item.

We have a no returns policy.

I'd like to exchange an item for another item.

What item would you like to exchange?

Typhus.

What problems are you having with this item?

It's typhus, and I don't want it.

Is it not working as intended?

No, it's working as intended, but it's a devastating disease.

What's the problem?

I brought a potato to this exchange, and I was hoping to get something that was either equivalent to a potato or better than a potato.

Typhus took generations to perfect.

Granted. I would not, however, describe it as "better than a potato." The potato also took generations to perfect; it is a highly portable, nutrient-rich carbohydrate, and if you

leave it alone in a kitchen, it will turn, unprompted, into
a plant that will produce more of itself. If you wanted to
power a clock, you could use the potato to help with that.
It is a versatile and wonderful tuber, and I deserve better
than typhus for it.

That's just your opinion, though.

No, it isn't. I think it is safe to say that all humans feel the
same way about the relative merits of potatoes and typhus.
If I were to go out into the street and shout "I have typhus
and a potato, which one do you want?" I can guarantee
right now what the response would be.

What would the response be?

"One of these things is a delicious rock you can eat! The
other one is a disease that is characterized by purple rash,
fevers, and delirium, which can be transmitted by rat
fleas!" Which do you think people are going to choose?

I'm fascinated to find out!

That guy over there got a horse! I want a horse. Or at the
very least, I would like my potato back.

We don't do returns at the Columbian Exchange.

What kind of exchange is this?

In the fine print, it says we're a very shitty exchange.

Would You Describe Yourselves as Normal Europeans? A Survey for New Arrivals

When they arrived in the area that would become the United States, the Pilgrims took this survey, I'm pretty sure.

1. **Would you describe yourselves as normal Europeans?**

    ○ Yes, if more Europeans were only willing to accept religion that is correct
    ○ No, because everyone else in Europe is a sinner whose ways are bad

2. **Choose THREE of the following phrases to describe yourselves:**

    ○ Sent because everyone back at home was so impressed
    ○ Weird cultists
    ○ Normal people seeking a better life
    ○ Fun-loving friends!
    ○ Birders who have collected every European bird and want to see more and better birds!

- ○ Members of the coveted 18–34 demographic
- ○ Convicts
- ○ Just here with the boat and going right back
- ○ Greg (put this only if your name is Greg)
- ○ Vikings who got started late

3. **Are you a cult?**
    (Please answer on the following 1–10 scale.)

1	2	3	4	5	6	7	8	9	10

Nobody has ever accused us of being in a cult.	*It's not a cult, really. We just feel very strongly everyone else is going to burn in fiery torment.*	*We're surprised when we meet anyone who doesn't immediately suggest we're a cult.*

4. **Are you fun?**

- ○ Yes—prayer is the highest fun
- ○ No—prayer is a grave responsibility

5. **What did people back home say about you?**

- ○ "Oh, those religious weirdos!"
- ○ "Ah, yes, we deported them."
- ○ "Sorry, we're too busy dealing with war and civil unrest. Go away."

6.   **Is religion important to your life?**

   ○ Yes, it is everything
   ○ Sure, but just the normal amount
      (normal being it's literally the only thing we think or
      talk about all the time)
   ○ No, my life means nothing without religion

7.   **Do you have anything to declare? Select from the
     following options:**

   ○ Disease
   ○ Genocide
   ○ Both disease and genocide

8.   **What is your anticipated departure date?
     (Please don't leave this blank!)**

   _____

   _____

9.   **You left it blank, didn't you.**

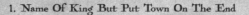

1. Name Of King But Put Town On The End

2. New [Place You Just Left]

3. Name Of Place You Just Left Without The Word New, Just To Confuse Everyone

4. If You Don't Come Up With Something It Will Autosave As New Town

5. Your Ethnic Group, Plural, But Put Boro On The End

6. Positive Or Neutral Noun (Fort, Haven) Describing The Place But Put New In Front

7. Name Of Different Monarch With -Ton On The End Just To Spice Things Up

8. Native American Name, But Misspelled

9. Greek For "The Condition Of Loving Brothers"

10. Generic Type Of Monarch But With -Ton Or -Ston On The End

11. Place From The Bible

12. Place From The Bible With New In Front

13. Phrase Meaning "Large Tits"

10

4 ← 3

12

YOUR NAME'S WOODS!
WHY NOT? BUT MAKE
THE WOODS LATIN
TO CONFUSE PEOPLE

8

6

2 ←

9 ←

NAME OF
QUEEN

5

WORD DESCRIBING
HOW MANY TIMES
THE QUEEN HAS
HAD SEX

1

11 ←

NAME OF MONARCH
BUT IN LATIN
JUST TO BE FANCY

7

NAME OF
MONARCH

N
W E
S

0   50   100 mi

Top Toys for Puritan Parents

The Puritans were strict religious types who descended upon New England in the 1620s and '30s. They wore somber dress and held draconian views on whether Sunday should be a funday—but they must have gotten their toys from somewhere.

Here at Puritan Parenting, we offer a variety of products to keep your little one on the right path! From the people who brought you 1690's best-selling *New-England Primer* and its multiplatinum nursery rhymes ("With Adam's Fall / We Sinned all" and "The Cat doth play / And after slay") come these new learning toys guaranteed to fire your child's imagination and instill in them a healthy fear of the damnation that yawns eternally beneath them.

Guess Who's Saved!: Fun game for all ages! Using yes or no questions, try to figure out which of the crowd of seemingly identical figures are among God's Elect—and which are doomed to eternal fire and brimstone! There's really no way of knowing! That's what would make this game so fun, if fun were not prohibited.

Memento Mori Mobile: This charming decoration will keep the inevitability of death constantly in your child's mind, featuring a tiny Sword of Damocles (real sword included) dangling by a single thread. Pull string plays "Dies Irae."

Plush Sinner: This fragile and easily damaged stuffed doll is meant for the hands of your angry child. The Sinner is flammable and vulnerable, and only grace can possibly preserve him! Fireplace not included.

Spider Being Dangled by a Thread: This companion toy for the Plush Sinner helps illustrate the same metaphor more vividly!

Calvin and Not Hobbes: A book of sermons by John Calvin. Un-comic, un-illustrated, unabridged. Suitable for all ages!

Unpacifier: The notion of being at peace even for a moment smacks of antinomian heresy. This wormwood-flavored pacifier will ensure your child is never, for a moment, allowed to feel complacent or at ease.

Putty: There is nothing silly about this putty. It is a plain, functional putty that can be used to imprint passages of scripture by pressing it firmly against the Bible, and is useless for any other purpose.

Yo: This would be a yo-yo if, once fallen, it could be called back again. But it cannot. Beseech your child never to let it fall! Keeps uppermost in her mind the wages of sin, which is hellfire eternal!

Elmo Who Delights in Nothing: This Elmo sits silently and contemplates his sinfulness. Do not seek to tickle him; this is folly.

Hot Wheels: These wheels are hot because of brimstone!

Difficult Bake Oven: Nothing good ought to be easy.

Where's the One Righteous Man for the Sake of Whom God Will Spare the City of Sodom from His Wrath?: His name is Waldo, and you can find him because he's wearing a little hat.

Cotton Mather: Spirit Hunter

The Mathers! They were definitely a family. They kicked around Massachusetts in the seventeenth century. Increase Mather was a preacher and, for a time, president of Harvard. Cotton Mather was a preacher, author, and bewildering individual who was on the right side of smallpox inoculation trials (pro) but on the wrong side of witch trials (also pro.) His grift was wandering around Massachusetts writing about people who thought they were experiencing witchcraft, and if he had access to the technology, I guarantee this would have taken the form of a ghost-hunting TV show.

MAN IN WIG: Hey I'm Cotton Mather, author of *Wonders of the Invisible World*. This is my father. His name is Increase. We're both Puritan ministers.

Shot of a dour-looking man with white hair standing proudly next to a slightly less dour-looking man with slightly less white hair. Behind them is a sign that reads "Falem Village, Population 500."

INCREASE: I don't want to be included in this.

COTTON: But I'm also an expert on the paranormal. And I'm here to help out these families by collecting spectral evidence about the witches that are giving them problems, using the most cutting-edge legal and theological wisdom 1690s New England has to offer.

New England Town, Day.

A buggy containing Cotton Mather and his team pulls up outside a modest wooden house. An older farmer in a somber black coat steps out and bows to Cotton Mather. Cotton bows back.

[b-roll] *Sheep stare incuriously at them from the middle distance.*

COTTON (VOICE-OVER): Everyone knows that witches exist. They're in the Bible. They're attested all over the world. Since ancient times. And I'm at the cutting edge of witch detection.

Montage: Cotton reading from the Bible. Cotton staring into a fireplace. Cotton looking intently at a toad.

COTTON: We've helped a lot of people.

The man leads Cotton inside to where his family is lined up dressed demurely in modest linsey-woolsey outfits.

FARMER: I'm so glad Cotton is here. We thought the neighbor was maybe a witch, and I was like, hold on, let's not get carried away here. Let's get someone with the experience to address the problem.

COTTON: I've got the best team in all New England. This is a learned doctor.

Learned Doctor is a man with an enormous white wig in a black ensemble with "F B I: Falem Body Inspector" stitched painstakingly on it by hand.

LEARNED DOCTOR: I am so excited to be on this team with Cotton. He is a legend, unlike witchcraft, which is not a legend at all and is just, you know, a true thing.

Shot of Learned Doctor standing in front of a stone wall, holding a big leather-bound volume and looking stern.

COTTON: Learned has read the *Malleus Maleficarum* cover to cover.

LEARNED DOCTOR: *Malleus Maleficarum* means "Hammer of Witches." It's just a great resource for identifying witches, you know? Super rigorous. I know all the signs that someone is a witch. So if you have any concerns, I'm the guy who can come in and shave the whole body and just, you know, check it over for witch's teats or other signs.

COTTON: Learned is a very thorough guy.

A very uncomfortable-looking woman stands naked in the center of a room as Learned and a group of other stern-looking men in black thoroughly examine her entire body.

COTTON: Most witches are women.

LEARNED DOCTOR: Yeah, fortunately or unfortunately Satan seems to be most tempting to the weaker sex, so I have to spend a lot of time checking them over. If you're not an expert or may not know what to look for, you can miss that there's a witch's teat right in front of you. Satan's amulet, tucked below the skin.

COTTON: I have learned so much from this guy.

LEARNED DOCTOR: Hard evidence is so important.

FARMER: (to camera) We are like 90 percent that our neighbor is a witch, but I didn't want to put her to death without applying the most rigorous expertise available.

FARMER'S WIFE: Our neighbor was here babysitting our son William. Apparently she nursed him, which was kind of out of line. We exchanged some words. And then after she left, William kept acting sad and weird. So our doctor said that the thing to do was to hang up his blanket in the corner all day long, and then at night, see if there was anything in it, and if there was, throw it into the fire.

COTTON: This is just classic advice. It sounds like they're in really good hands.

FARMER'S WIFE: And we looked, and there was a TOAD in it.

FARMER: The toad got loose. We had to chase it around the room.

COTTON: Wow.

FARMER'S WIFE: Finally we caught the toad and held it into the fire with the tongs. And it made a horrible popping noise and flashed like gunpowder, and then it vanished!

COTTON: Wow.

FARMER: But that's not all.

FARMER'S WIFE: The witch-neighbor's nephew told us that he saw her that week, and she was scorched all over like a toad that had been put into a fire would be scorched.

COTTON: Incredible. And are you still being affected?

FARMER: Both our children are now lame and have to go about on crutches.

COTTON: Wow. On what side?

FARMER: It varies.

COTTON: (to camera) So the protocol in a case like this is you pay a visit to the suspected witch.

Shaky shot of a shack from a far distance. A voice can be heard shouting, "I AM NOT A WITCH! THIS IS PRIVATE PROPERTY! THIS IS PRIVATE PROPERTY!"

A turkey emerges from the bushes and runs toward the camera.

MUFFLED VOICES: Yeah, we got maybe a familiar, some kind of familiar?

COTTON: The next step was to really do an interview with the children, see what kind of sorcery you're dealing with.

Footage of the children. One of them pretends to vomit into his clenched fist, then opens it to produce a coin and some nails. Cotton nods thoughtfully.

COTTON: They had a lot going on. Sometimes they were lame on one side. Sometimes on the other side. I would try to get them to read the Bible, but they would say, "The witch says I am not to read that." Or I would point out the word *Satan* to them, and they would say, "I love Satan now because of this woman who is a witch." Pretty incontrovertible stuff.

LEARNED: One of them saw an invisible mouse run into the fire, and then there was a really big FLASH, which we all saw, even though the mouse was invisible.

Title: REENACTMENT.

Shot of everyone staring intently at the fire. Something goes CRACKLE in the fire, and everyone points.

COTTON: Lots of remarkable providences of that nature. It reminded me a lot of one of my first cases, one I handled all by myself. There was a family who had a daughter, and she clearly was in thrall to Satan in some way, because when I would read to her from my dad's book, she hated it.

LEARNED: Everyone knows that Increase Mather's books are all amazing, and only a witch would not want to hear every word of those awesome texts.

COTTON: And they tried to give her an apple to eat, but she didn't eat it, but then she ate it later.

LEARNED: Classic.

COTTON: And she didn't want to read the Bible but did want to read from a book of popular jests, and she would laugh out loud at a lot of them.

LEARNED: Such a bad sign.

COTTON: Also she rode up the stairs on an invisible horse.* So with that under my belt, I knew what we were dealing with.

LEARNED: There was another woman in the neighborhood who was also accused of being a witch. She had a Satan's amulet on her body. A farmer managed to break her window with one of his carts, and she yelled at him.

Title: REENACTMENT

Shot of a woman yelling, "GET OFF MY PROPERTY! I AM A WITCH!"

LEARNED: And then after that . . . all his other carts were fine, but the cart that had run into the window kept getting stuck at gates. They had to park it and unload it very far away, and everybody who helped to unload it had a bad time.

COTTON: We were all like, nothing explains this.

LEARNED: The cart was having big problems. And we were like, how can this be happening?? Could this cart have been damaged in some way by striking the window? Or isn't it more likely that this is witchcraft?

COTTON: She also yelled at another man, and then his horses died, and he got lice.

LEARNED: Not just the normal amount of lice but like a whole lot of lice, really big mean ones.

COTTON: Had to burn two whole suits to get rid of them.

---

* This did happen! As did the other examples. All of which honestly seem fair and relatable except for the invisible horse situation, which I want to know more about.

LEARNED: Dead giveaway.

COTTON: Witchcraft was the only possible explanation.

Group of somber, black-hatted men stand gathered to hear from Cotton.

COTTON: Yeah, we've had a great week here studying all these mysterious providences, and we've applied all our expertise and come to the conclusion we were hoping to avoid: it's definitely witchcraft.

The men all nod somberly.

MAN: Has there ever been an episode when you discovered it . . . wasn't witchcraft?

COTTON: (shaking his head sadly) No.

A Spider Objects to Jonathan Edwards

Jonathan Edwards was a preacher during the Great Awakening, a religious revival that sprang up in the eighteenth century in response to concerns that people had gotten too into Reason and were devoting fewer and fewer hours every day to going around crippled by anxiety about their eternal souls. He memorably delivered a sermon titled "Sinners in the Hands of an Angry God" (pretty much what it says on the label), in which he likened the plight of a sinful man to that of a spider or loathsome insect being held over a flame. I can't imagine that everyone hearing it was pleased.

DEAREST SIRS AND ALL THOSE WHOM IT MAY
CONCERN
IT HAS COST ME MANY PAINS TO WRITE THESE
WORDS SINCE I HAD TO SPELL IT ALL OUT LETTER
BY LETTER WITH MY WHOLE BODY USING FLUID
FROM MY SPINNERETS AND AT ONE POINT A DOG
RAN THROUGH AND RUINED IT ALL

I WILL BE BRIEF
JONATHAN EDWARDS HAS BESMIRCHED MY NAME
AND THE NAMES OF MANY OTHER SPIDERS
WE ARE ALL AS GOOD AS ANY OF GOD'S CREATURES
I WAS SITTING THERE IN THE CENTER OF MY WEB

MINDING MY OWN BUSINESS
WATCHING THE WEB FOR THE ARRHYTHMIC
VIBRATIONS THAT INDICATE THAT A FLY IS
PRESENT SO THAT I MAY SEIZE THE FLY AND STAB
HIM MANY TIMES WITH MY VENOM
WHEN I HEARD HIM
"THE GOD THAT HOLDS YOU OVER THE PIT OF
HELL, MUCH AS ONE HOLDS A SPIDER OR SOME
LOATHSOME INSECT OVER THE FIRE, ABHORS YOU"
PICTURE MY SURPRISE TO HEAR MYSELF
MENTIONED AND SINGLED OUT IN THIS SERMON
I AM NOT A CONGREGANT OF REVEREND EDWARDS
NOR, FRANKLY, AFTER THIS SERMON, WOULD I BE
INCLINED TO BECOME ONE
I AM JUST A SPIDER TRYING MY BEST TO LIVE MY LIFE
I DON'T MAKE ANY PRETENSE TO BEING HOLIER
THAN ANYONE ELSE
BUT I WORK HARD FOR MY FAMILY
I TRY VERY HARD TO PUT DEAD FLY INTO THE
MOUTHS OF MY THOUSANDS OF SPIDERLINGS
I'M NOT ASHAMED OF WHO I AM, AND IF THE ONLY
WAY REVEREND JONATHAN EDWARDS KNOWS TO
MAKE HIS LISTENERS FEAR THE WAGES OF SIN IS TO
INSULT ME, I FEEL EMBARRASSED ON HIS BEHALF
I AM A VALUED MEMBER OF MY COMMUNITY
I LIKE TO THINK THAT I PROVIDE A SERVICE AND
THAT WHAT I DO IS HONEST
GENERATIONS OF US HAVE LIVED AND DIED ON
THIS PLOT OF LAND
AND I HOPE MY CHILDREN AND THEIR CHILDREN
WILL CONTINUE THE TRADITION OF KEEPING FLIES

OUT OF THIS CONGREGATIONALIST CHURCH
BUT PERHAPS WE WON'T NOW
FURTHERMORE I AM NOT A LOATHSOME INSECT
I AM AN ARACHNID.
GOOD DAY SIR

Listen My Children and You Shall Hear of the Midnight Ride of Paul Revere and Also Samuel Prescott Who Was There Too Even If His Name Doesn't Rhyme as Well

If writing huge amounts of tremendously popular, patriotic historical poetry in the nineteenth century was wrong, Henry Wadsworth Longfellow did not want to be right. He gave us "Paul Revere's Ride." He gave us "Song of Hiawatha." He gave us "The Courtship of Miles Standish." He gave us the phrase "whom the gods would destroy they first make mad"! These were all big hits back in the day, to the point that he became the only American poet whose bust you can see in Westminster Abbey's Poets' Corner!

Edgar Allan Poe apparently thought he was derivative, but compared to Edgar Allan Poe, who wasn't?

One problem (of many!) with a lot of these poems is that they are not strictly historically accurate! I have a theory about why. Longfellow, you see, was a lyric poet, which meant things had to rhyme and have a certain rhythm. This early draft of "Paul Revere's Ride" suggests some of the difficulties he would have faced.

✳

Listen, my children, and you shall hear
Of the midnight ride of Paul Revere,
On the eighteenth of April, in Seventy-Five:
Hardly a man is now alive
Who remembers that famous day and year.
But 'ere we very much further go
Another fact that you ought to know
A fact I'm not hesitant to reveal
A fact I make no effort to conceal
Is that also along for the ride that night
A ride that history keeps in sight
Was someone named Samuel Prescott.
I'm including him in the poem too!
It's important, you see, because of the two
He was the one who actually made
The ride to Concord, where he bade
The warning sound and the troops prepare
It was important that he was there
And I will not stint—let me now be clear
Though his name is nothing like Paul Revere
A name that rhymes with so many things
A name with music, that really sings
A name that rhymes with both *dear* and *steer*
Appear, and *bier*, too, and also *beer*
You must admit, I am sure, this man
Makes it so easy to rhyme and scan.
I could write Paul Revere odes all day
Though I'm not biased in any way
But it is true that he's got a name

That quite well suits to poetic fame!
Which is not a thing I could say as well
Of a man whose name is a funeral knell
When it comes to rhyming, not what we've best got
You know the man I mean: Samuel Prescott.
Hmm, this is going to be a problem, I think.
Not that I'm less than tickled pink
To write of these men and their storied ride
A ride that echoes and stirs our pride
Through the ages long, one that men must praise
As long as our country's flag we raise.
Ahem. Upon that night dark and clear
Away rode wonderful Paul Revere
Rhyming so nicely, he rode his steed
To aid our country in hour of need
He was dressed in a coat of green
A color that blended with such a scene
Then Samuel—our friend, you know, Mr. Prescott
Went to the drawer and his finest vest got
And the hue of that vest was orange.
I'm sorry, I don't think I can do this.
Listen my children and you shall hear
Of the midnight ride of Paul Revere
And also someone named William Dawes
Who 'scaped the lobsterbacks' loathsome jaws
AND CERTAINLY NOBODY ELSE AT ALL
As far as anyone can recall
Don't look it up! Just listen well!
I have a midnight ride to tell.
And who remembers those far-off days?

Let them be lost in our memory's haze!
If a man was there I did not address
Just know the rhymes would have been a mess
Don't mention—you know who, Samuel Pres
Cott.

The Hour Men

Much has been written about the exploits of the Minute Men, the American civilian militias who swore to be ready in a minute to help fight the British during the Revolutionary War. This seems made up to me, and I refuse to believe in it. People simply can't be ready in a minute. Here, I think, is a more likely account of how things would have gone: the recently unearthed diary of the most famous Hour Man, Nathaniel Hancock.

June 16, 1775, 3 PM

The call for aid is up! Bunker Hill is going to be attacked, and we men are all being mustered. They came house to house telling everyone to get ready. "Terrific," I said. "It will not take me more than one minute to get ready."

"Good," Benjamin said, "because we are really serious about this one-minute thing, and we are going to be marching pretty much immediately."

"Absolutely!" I said. "This is the hour of fate!" I put on my most fierce-looking coat, buttoning each button with care, and gathered all the supplies I might need.

"Are you ready, Nathaniel?" my wife Bess inquired, glancing out the window. "All the Minute Men have assembled in the square, and they are about to march."

I told her that I was ready, which was essentially true, but then I remembered that we might need snacks.

"The Minute Men are leaving!" Bess said.

"That is fine!" I said. "I am ready to go!" which was true, although I was engaged in slicing carrots and placing them into a linen sack so that if we needed to have carrots when we got to Bunker Hill, we would not have to slice them there.

"Nathaniel," Benjamin said, "are you ready? We are marching right now, but if you are almost ready, we can wait."

"I am almost ready," I said. "It will take me one minute tops to get ready."

"That is what you said nigh twenty minutes ago," Benjamin said.

"Well, I'm ready now," I said.

"You don't have your musket," my wife said.

"I am ready," I said to Benjamin, "I just need to find where I put my musket."

"Nathaniel," Benjamin said, "we cannot wait around for you to find where you put your musket if that isn't top-of-mind information for you right now."

"It is top-of-mind information for me right now," I said. "It is definitely in the house somewhere, and I know I put it somewhere special where I would remember it."

"Nathaniel," Benjamin said, "we are going now."

"I am completely ready once I find my musket!" I said. "I have narrowed down the location of my musket to three possible places."

"Okay," Benjamin said, "we're leaving."

"I just need to put on my boots and grab my musket," I said.

"You don't even have your boots on?" Benjamin inquired.

"I have footwear on," I said, "but it occurred to me that we will probably be walking, and I'm going to want to be in boots."

"Yes," Benjamin said. "This was all on the list I gave out earlier."

"I know," I said. "I read the list, and I put it right next to my musket."

Benjamin sighed heavily.

"Are you still waiting around for this guy?" somebody else said, in what I thought was an unnecessarily unpleasant tone.

"What you should do," my wife said to Benjamin in an urgent, soft voice that I believe she thought I could not hear, "is tell him an hour earlier than you actually need him to be there."

"I can't do that," Benjamin said. "We are Minute Men, and our whole thing is that we have to be ready in a minute to go to a location that wasn't previously specified. Anyway, we are going to march now, and we will have to catch up with you and your husband later."

And with that they marched off, a cloud of dust rising in their wake.

June 16, 1775, 4 PM

I am entirely ready to leave for Bunker Hill now, but I wonder if I hadn't better wait until the morning. Probably if the British are there, they will still be there later. If they are having a battle, I don't want to interrupt them in the middle of it, which I imagine would be pretty awkward. They might already be firing their muskets, and they might not know that it was I, Nathaniel Hancock, arriving with carrots and other assorted forms of aid and succor, and they might do something they regretted. Bess thinks I had better go because people will pass remarks, but if they win, that will prove that my presence was not necessary, and if they lose, it will be a relief that I was not there. She does not wish them to think me a coward. She would not think me a coward, she explained, but other people might think it. Anyway, I am leaving now as soon as I put on my boots.

June 17, 1775, 7 PM

I have just gotten back from Bunker Hill! It was a little awkward as I ran into everyone on the road as they were coming back. I had only gotten about halfway there when I saw a great column of dust coming down the road. It was everyone who had set out, mostly, although some of them had wounds that they did not have before, and I did not see Benjamin at all. I tried to blend in to the group because that seemed less disruptive than waving them down and having to explain where I had been. I fell into step and marched along with them as unobtrusively as I could. A newspaper writer came and asked us about the recent engagement, and I said loudly, "Bunker Hill was the spot! I will never forget being there at Bunker Hill! What a battle the Battle of Bunker Hill was!" and then I offered him a sliced carrot. Everyone around me was looking at me, and after the writer left, they made some very stinging remarks about how if I had been at the engagement, I would know that it was at Breed's Hill and not at Bunker. There was really nothing to say after that, and the march back into town was quite long. I am not sure if I am welcome in the Minute Men any longer.

50 States of Grey

*Excerpts from a never-published erotic history of the
United States that got sprinkled in here by mistake*

"Give it to me," Patrick Henry gasped.

"What?"

"Liberty. Or death. One of the two."

The Virginia House of Delegates shifted uncomfort-
ably. "There has to be another way of phrasing that,"
said George Washington, who was there.

John and Abigail Adams
Try Sexting

The second U.S. president, John "Obnoxious, Suspected, and Unpopular" Adams, and Abigail "Remember the Ladies" Adams spent good chunks of their marriage on opposite sides of the Atlantic Ocean, a situation that seems ripe for some kind of effort to keep things spicy. We have the rest of their correspondence. Why not this too?

Peace field ("old house"), Quincy Mass., Apr. 1st, 1778
Dear John,
What are you wearing?

Hotel de Valois, Paris, France, May 21st, 1778
My Dearest Friend,
I am wearing a good thick woolen coat of sound construction as well as my customary stockings, long linen shirt, and knee breeches. It is a brisk, chill day here in Paris, yet as I stamp and rub my hands in the cold, or shove them more deeply into my stout brown coat's Pockets, I am Past by many a man clad gaily like a field in riot with sunflowers. Such are the exigencies of fashion here! I feel a very Wren amidst so many Peacocks.

Peace field, June 8th, 1778
Dear John,
I delighted very much in your description of the Fashions! I

must be candid, John: I inquired as to what you were wearing in the hopes that we might engage in simulated coitus via letter. I apologize if that was unclear, in case you should wish to alter your description of what attire you are wearing.

Hotel de Valois, June 23rd, 1778
My Dearest Friend,
Ah! What would be the benefit of such an exchange? It seems to me that sheets of cotton and sheets of parchment offer very different possibilities for marital disportment.

Peace field, July 7th, 1778
Dear John,
Here, John, I have drawn a map. You are indicated with an X, and I am indicated with another X, and we may see by examining this map closely that you are on one continent whereas I am on another continent, so any pursuit involving cotton sheets, however desirable, is, alas, impossible. Paper sheets are what must pass between us. I will now attempt to describe what I am wearing, that you may carry my picture in the glass of your mind. I am attired in a woolen gown and a cap of a stiff linen material, as well as five petticoats, my bustle, and my customary stays. I was wearing stockings, but I am not wearing them any longer.

Hotel de Valois, July 31, 1778
Dear Abigail,
The map was very helpful. I shall endeavor to apply myself to this enterprise with a will. I see that you are wearing five petticoats. I hope that soon you shall be wearing merely four!

Peace field, August 13th, 1778
Dear John,
The cows do not thrive, and we are having great difficulty about the farm. Also, I have done some arithmetic, and at the rate our letters travel, it is going to be Christmas before I get down to one petticoat, so I have taken the liberty of removing all five of the petticoats in order to expedite the proceedings somewhat. I hope this shall not be taken as undue forwardness, but you must concede that one petticoat a month would be sorely trying. Suppose that one of our letters should be lost at sea; we might be left in a great ambiguity and confusion as to how many petticoats remained, and then we might be mired for several months endeavoring to remove petticoats that had already been removed. I seek to avoid such a quagmire. What is the state of your own attire?

Hotel de Valois, August 20th, 1778
Dear Abigail,
I have not heard from you since my last letter and hope the cows thrive and that all on the farm is easy and pleasant. All is well here. The sun shines brightly upon your John, who longs for you as the Magnet is reported to long for certain Metals and perhaps also Electricity in a metaphor drawn from those thrilling experiments which I as yet imperfectly comprehend.

I am still attired in my stockings and breeches. I hope that soon you shall be wearing merely three petticoats!

Peace field, September 5th, 1778
Dear John,
I see from your last letter that you did not receive my last letter. As I feared, we are now in a quagmire: my last letter noted

that it would be imprudent to remove merely a single petticoat with each letter and therefore I took the liberty of removing the remaining four, but as you are unaware of it I suppose I had better revert to three petticoats.

Hotel de Valois, September 7th, 1778
My Dearest Friend,
It grieves me to hear about your struggles with the cows. I could wish you many a pleasanter avocation than that one. It is prudent, what you have thought about the petticoats, and in keeping with the spirit of your suggestion, I am removing my thick woolen greatcoat of sound construction.

Peace field, September 23rd, 1778
Dear John,
I believe that you are receiving my missives out of order and I think we had better halt proceedings until we can sort out this matter. How many petticoats am I wearing, exactly, in your mind? I will make no further movement on the petticoat front until I have heard from you.

Hotel de Valois, October 1st, 1778
My Dearest Friend,
Now I have removed my long shirt!

Peace field, October 20th, 1778
Dear John,
I see from your most recent missive that you did not receive either of my last letters, and now we have entered into the very quagmire I most dreaded, where an indeterminate number of petticoats hover between us across the roaring Atlantic. I

believe I must put a halt to things until we can ascertain how many petticoats you believe me to be wearing. Please do not attempt to continue the proceedings until we have settled on a number.

Hotel de Valois, October 31st, 1778
My Dearest Friend,
It is either three petticoats or zero petticoats.

Peace field, November 13th, 1778
Dear John,
Yes, this is the matter I am seeking to resolve. Shall we settle on zero, then?

Hotel de Valois, November 14th, 1778
My Dearest Friend,
I have received no letter from you. I pray that all is well with you. It is either three petticoats or zero petticoats.

Peace field, November 18th, 1778
Dear John,
When I saw that the ship containing my last packet of letters had foundered, I feared the worst. Let us settle upon zero. Well did Shakespeare write "trust not to rotten planks"! I miss you.

Hotel de Valois, December 10th, 1778
My Dearest Friend,
I rejoice that you are in safe keeping! Now that we have settled upon zero petticoats, is my greatcoat on or off? And what of my shirt? Ought I to set about keeping a log to make matters clearer? I may ask Benjamin Franklin for his advice upon this

matter; it seems an area in which he would be Possessed of knowledge and might offer a sound Recommendation.

Peace field, Jan 1st, 1779
Dear John,
A new year dawns! Much time has passed since we began this correspondence. I cannot say that it offers much to recommend itself, but perhaps it will gain in interest once we have made our way through this morass of petticoats. In honor of this milestone, I shall take the liberty of removing my stays altogether.

John Adams's Lodgings, France, March 23rd, 1779!
Dear Abigail Adams,
I, John Adams, your husband, am completely naked and stand ready for action. I am wild and cannot be Governed! My Ardour may only be quenched by being Doused, as a Conflagration would be quenched by the many divers Water Buckets of the tremendous volunteer fire brigade organized by Benjamin Franklin in Philadelphia, the first of its nature in that place! We shall kindle one another's Eagerness like a Kite being struck by Lightning (as might occur if a man of Genius fixed it in his mind to perform a Worthy Experiment). Place a Basket over your head to obscure all the Deficiency of Fluid in neck & Visage that has ensued as a consequence of Age, and let us have at it! And we must spare a thought for Benjamin Franklin, a worthy man!

Hotel de Valois, March 24th, 1779
My Dearest Friend,
DO NOT OPEN THE MOST RECENT LETTER IT WAS SENT IN ERROR BY BENJAMIN FRANKLIN WHO WAS FRANKLY NOT THE MAN TO CONSULT IN THIS

MATTER AND TO WHOM I HAVE COMPOSED STERN
WORDS OF REPROOF

Hotel de Valois, March 26th, 1779
My Dearest Friend,
I am sending another letter urging you against opening the last
letter in case the ship bearing my last letter saying not to open
the first letter should have suffered any mischance! My Dearest
Abigail the shame & mortification & horror that overcame me
when I saw that F— had put his missive in the post cannot be
described. I pray that you may forgive me one day.

Hotel de Valois, March 30, 1779
My Dearest Friend,
This is another letter beseeching you not to open my most
recent letter, unless you did open it and found it was a letter
urging you not to open another letter, in which case, that is
fine. I am not talking about that letter, I am talking about a
different letter. Any letter whose contents are anything other
than urging you not to open a letter ought not to be opened.
Oh dear

Peace field, April 14th, 1779
Dear John,
I did not for a moment believe you guilty of the missive whose
arrival you so dreaded; the penmanship was entirely unlike
yours and its praise of Benjamin Franklin far too liberal to be
mistaken for one of your productions. It shewed an admirable
directness, I suppose, but offered little else to recommend it.
I doubted very much whether you would urge me to place a
Basket over my Face to increase your corporal enjoyment.

Hotel de Valois, May 9th, 1779
My Dearest Friend,
O the agonies of shame & horror that have wracked me when I consider what missive passed from the pen of Franklin to your waiting hands cannot be exaggerated. I fear it has somewhat doused my enthusiasm for this venture.
Though I rue the cause, I return to Boston next Month! In the words of the bard, let lips do what Hands do (poorly, in these missives) and forgo any further attempts at correspondence of this nature.

Peace field, August 30th, 1779
Dear John,
It was very good to see you.

Peace field, Sept. 1, 1779
My Dearest Friend,
It was very good to see you!

An Oral History of the Constitutional Convention

We know that the 1787 Constitutional Convention occurred from May to September, the most fun months to be in Philadelphia wearing layers. We also know the contours of the discussion because of James Madison, who took extensive notes. He later went on to become the fourth (and shortest) president, and he was the sitting commander in chief when the British came through and burned the White House, a distinction that will be hard to replicate even if a shorter person one day becomes president. Usually, the best way to find out about an event attended by and involving lots of people is to interview them all years after the fact. So that's what I did.

GOUVERNEUR MORRIS: The Constitutional Convention was great, but I wish more people had taken notes. I kept seeing James Madison taking notes, but I never knew what he was writing down. I think we should have had another guy also taking notes, because how can we know that what James Madison says we said is what we said? I said, "Hey there, James, what are you writing down?" and he just sort of nodded at me. We don't want to wind up in a situation where we know what people said only because of what James Madison wrote down.

MADISON: I kept very accurate notes. You need have no fears upon that score.

FROM MADISON'S NOTES: *Gouverneur Morris was silent for the entire duration of the Constitutional Convention, except once when he said that he respected me.*

GOUVERNEUR MORRIS: I said lots of things. Every morning as I came in I would say, "Madison, write down that I said you suck."

MADISON: I only wrote down things that were important.

GOUVERNEUR MORRIS: I said, "Madison, you suck! If we ever agree that there should be an office called President, and if you ever are elected to it, you will be the shortest and worst."

FROM MADISON'S NOTES: *Gouverneur Morris expressed support for the presidency as a concept, though as was usual for this man, who posterity ought to know smelled weird and had the wrong number of legs, he did so very incoherently.*

FRANKLIN: I think Madison's notes are broadly accurate. I also tried taking notes, but I believe his were better.

FROM FRANKLIN'S NOTES: *A. Hamilton spoke at length on his idea for a new form of government. Room very hot. Strange humming and buzzing suggests new idea for musical instrument.*

List of Things One Might Make Harmoniums Out of Besides Glass: metal perhaps? Wood polished to a sheen?

Things to Do: respond to admirer's letter, disown son, have hat mended

MORRIS: To be fair, I tried taking notes briefly, just to show James Madison, but I got bored midway through after General Washington said a sixth time that he wasn't worthy of the great honor being bestowed upon him by the American people. I zoned out and drew an enormous rabbit the size of a man.

GEORGE WASHINGTON: I was highly sensible of the enormous burden and responsibility that had been placed in my hands by the convention, and endeavored to explain that I would execute it to the utmost of my abilities, unworthy though I was.

FROM MADISON'S NOTES: *General Washington expressed once again his sense of the enormous burden that had been placed on his shoulders, unworthy though he was, and vowed to discharge this grave responsibility with all the skill that lay within his power. He stressed the sentiment very much.*

MORRIS: I became obsessed with the rabbit. Would a man-sized rabbit dress like a man, or go unclad? What manner of hat would he sport? I drew many hats for the rabbit and passed them around the back row of delegates to have them vote on which seemed best and most likely.

FRANKLIN: Madison didn't record that the best day of the convention was when Gouverneur Morris drew an anatomically correct man-rabbit and lady-rabbit and had us vote on what clothes they should wear.

MORRIS: Dr. Franklin became obsessed with the rabbit in his turn and demanded that I should make a dog in the same manner, with clothes likewise, but then the room was split as to how many legs his pants ought to have.

HAMILTON: The dog's pants should have four legs. It is self-evident, and I have an eighty-nine-page treatise that shall explain why!

MORRIS: I started drawing cartoons just to calm everyone down. The dog thing was tearing us apart.

ELBRIDGE GERRY: He drew me as a lizard. I said, "That would be a great shape for a congressional district!"

MORRIS: In retrospect I was sorry to have caused the distraction because while we were all focused on the rabbit, the chair asked if anyone had any ideas for a better system of voting than an electoral college, and nobody said anything.

FROM MADISON'S NOTES: *We determined upon the formation of an electoral college with little objection. Slight disturbance in back of room caused by the aforementioned Mr. Gouv. Morris was quelled.*

MORRIS: I said, aw, I would have said something, but Madison said it was time to move on to once again entwine slavery more deeply into the framework of this nation.

FROM MADISON'S NOTES: *Gouverneur Morris as usual said nothing, but indicated by a gesture that he approved of my wisdom.*

MORRIS: I just really wish we had had more people taking notes.

The Original Plan for the Federalist Papers

After the Constitutional Convention, it was necessary to convince people to ratify the resulting Constitution. That was why James Madison, Alexander Hamilton, and John Jay decided to write the Federalist Papers under the name Publius—a set of pseudonymous publications anticipating the difficulties and objections people would have to the Constitution and defending it against them. They published their arguments in a series of eighty-five separate essays.

What no one knows (because, in the strictest, most literal sense, there is no evidence whatsoever that it happened) is that Hamilton thought it would be more exciting for readers if there were a plot to keep them coming back week after week. "What is going to keep them tuning in?" he asked. "These are way too episodic! This is a serialized form, and we are doing nothing with it." He spent many nights haranguing Madison and Jay about the main character. "We need to get people into this Publius guy so they invest in him and want to know why they should care about what he thinks about the Constitution!" Eventually he convinced the others to at least try to map out the basic plot, but for some reason Jay and Madison ultimately nixed the idea.

Federalist 1: General Introduction. The Importance of the Subject. Publius will offer public arguments. General plan of the series, to show the utility of the Union to political prosperity, etc. Publius saves a cat from a tree so we know we're rooting for him.

Federalist 2: Concerning Dangers from Foreign Force and Influence. We meet Publius's roommates.

Federalist 3: The Same Subject Continued. Publius makes a discovery that changes everything.

Federalist 4: The Same Subject Continued. A bottle episode where Publius gets stuck in a stagecoach with two rival armonica players. (John Jay's idea! He can write this.)

Federalist 5: The Same Subject Continued. Publius hears the Articles of Confederation making a weird sound and goes to investigate.

Federalist 6: Concerning Dangers from Dissensions Between the States. Publius opens a door to find the Articles of Confederation standing over the dead bodies of his parents.

Federalist 7: The Same Subject Continued. A grief-stricken Publius finds himself in a fight for his life against the Articles of Confederation.

Federalist 8: Consequences of Hostility Between the States. The Articles of Confederation escape from Publius—and from justice!—by leaping onto a speeding horse and fleeing into the night.

Federalist 9: The Union as a Safeguard Against Domestic Faction and Insurrection. Publius vows revenge against the Articles of Confederation.

Federalist 10: The Same Subject Continued. Publius gets a mysterious letter from someone claiming to know the Articles of Confederation's whereabouts.

Federalist 11: The Utility of the Union in Respect to Commercial Relations and a Navy. Publius goes on a boat ride.

Federalist 12: The Utility of the Union in Respect to Revenue. Publius arrives at the last known location of the Articles of Confederation.

Federalist 13: Advantage of the Union in Respect to Economy in Government. Publius bursts in—but the Articles of Confederation are already gone, their hideaway abandoned. But someone is there: a Bill of Rights.

Federalist 14: Objections to the Proposed Constitution from Extent of Territory Answered. Publius and the Bill of Rights realize they have a common enemy. But can Bill trust him?

Federalist 15: The Insufficiency of the Present Confederation to Preserve the Union. Publius tells Bill of Rights what the Articles of Confederation did to his family.

Federalist 16: Flashback to Publius and his family in happier times, made bittersweet by the knowledge we now possess.

50 States of Grey

"Put it in," Patrick Henry whimpered.

"Its presence is already implied," James Madison said. He was gasping in the Virginia heat, although he was of course also from Virginia, but just because you are from a place does not mean you cannot gasp in its heat. His wife Dolley, however, was from North Carolina.

"I need you to put it in," Patrick Henry moaned. "Virginia needs it." They were on the brink of completion. They had been there for twenty-five days, eating nothing but sandwiches.

Madison was sweating heavily from the labor, as well as from the copious contemporaneous notes that he was, as always, engaged in setting down. "Virginia doesn't know what it needs."

"Are you going to put it in, or aren't you?" Henry grunted. "This should be easy, Jemmy. We want it. Our constitution can take it."

"Yes," Madison grunted. "Okay. You win. I promise. There will be a Bill of Rights."

"That's all I was holding out for," Patrick Henry panted.

"Then will you ratify it?"

"Yes." Henry gasped. "Yes. Yes!"

Federalist 17: The Same Subject Continued. Bill tells Publius what the Articles of Confederation did to his best friend Daniel Shays.

Federalist 18: The Same Subject Continued. Bill and Publius decide they'll be stronger together. Or will they? Ask Alexander Hamilton for his thoughts on this!

Federalist 19: The Same Subject Continued. Publius meets a beautiful woman who asks for his help.

Federalist 20: The Same Subject Continued. Publius can't say no to a beautiful woman who asks for his help.

Federalist 21: Other Defects of the Present Confederation. An illustration of the beautiful woman asking for Publius's help.

Federalist 22: The Same Subject Continued. For subscribers who promise to ratify the Constitution, this one includes a much more detailed illustration of the beautiful woman where you can see *everything* (both ankles).

Federalist 23: The Necessity of a Government as Energetic as the One Proposed to the Preservation of the Union. The beautiful woman makes one request of Publius: to find the Articles of Confederation and kill them.

Federalist 24: The Powers Necessary to the Common Defense Further Considered. She introduces Publius to a wise old man who will serve as his mentor.

Federalist 25: The Same Subject Continued. Publius training montage.

Federalist 26: The Idea of Restraining the Legislative Authority in Regard to the Common Defense Considered. Publius, under his mentor's guidance, travels back in time to ancient Athens to observe an alternative form of government in action.

Federalist 27: The Same Subject Continued. Publius meets his hero Socrates.

Federalist 28: The Same Subject Continued. Socrates is sentenced to death, and Publius has to get him out of there fast!

Federalist 29: Concerning the Militia. Publius and Socrates must evade an angry band of hoplites.

Federalist 30: Concerning the General Power of Taxation. Publius and Socrates make it back to the present, not a moment too soon.

Federalist 31: The Same Subject Continued. Socrates marvels at the conveniences of the present day, but all is not as it seems.

Federalist 32: The Same Subject Continued. The world is not as Publius left it.

Federalist 33: The Same Subject Continued. Publius realizes his actions in the past have actually altered the present timeline.

Federalist 34: The Same Subject Continued. Socrates tells Publius that he must take him back to the past and leave him to face his fate.

Federalist 35: The Same Subject Continued. Socrates and Publius have a tearful farewell.

Federalist 36: The Same Subject Continued. Publius returns to the present, his heart breaking. All that remains of his adventure is a coin Socrates gave him to pay the god of healing.

Federalist 37: Concerning the Difficulties of the Convention in Devising a Proper Form of Government. Publius, still reeling from the loss of Socrates, dives into his vendetta against the Articles of Confederation.

Federalist 38: Incoherence of the Objections to the New Plan Exposed. John Jay here! I'm taking over the Publius arc for the next couple of issues!

Federalist 39: Conformity of the Plan to Republican Principles. Publius gets bitten by a strange insect. It's probably nothing.

Federalist 40: The Powers of the Convention to Form a Mixed Government Examined and Sustained. It's not nothing. Publius can't sleep. At night, he glows.

Federalist 41: General View of the Powers Conferred by the Constitution. Publius can look through walls now.

Federalist 42: The Powers Conferred by the Constitution Further Considered. Publius can look through not just walls but people. The world's skin is peeling back all around him.

Federalist 43: The Same Subject Continued. Publius feels restless, itchy.

Federalist 44: Restrictions on the Authority of the Several States. Publius looks at John Hanson, the president under the Articles of Confederation, and *he can see the subcutaneous tissue and the humors.*

Federalist 45: The Alleged Danger from the Powers of the Union to the State Governments Considered. A dull horror starts to gnaw at Publius as his eyes peel away all the comfortable coverings of the world.

Federalist 46: The Influence of the State and Federal Governments Compared. Publius doesn't want to see any deeper.

Federalist 47: The Particular Structure of the New Government and Distribution of Power Among Its Different Parts. At night, Publius lies awake and stares through his closed eyelids. Sleep eludes him.

Federalist 48: These Departments Should Not Be So Far Separated as to Have No Constitutional Control over Each Other. Publius tells his most trusted friend that he has started to see below the skin of John Hanson and that he doesn't like what he sees there. How much deeper beneath the skin of John Hanson will Publius's eyes be forced to go?

Federalist 49: Method of Guarding Against the Encroachments of Any One Department of Government by Appealing to the People Through a Convention. Publius locks himself in a dark room underground, desperate for the agony of too much sight to end.

Federalist 50: Periodic Appeals to the People Considered. Even in the deep fastness of the stone where he is concealed, Publius can see a light creeping in just at the edges of his vision. Soon there is light everywhere.

Federalist 51: The Structure of the Government Must Furnish the Proper Checks and Balances Between the Different Departments. Publius screams and screams.

Federalist 52: The House of Representatives. Publius screams and screams.

Federalist 53: The Same Subject Continued. Publius screams and screams.

Federalist 54: The Apportionment of Members Among States. Hamilton again: Jay, what in hell is this? Jay here: Really glad you're back because I didn't know how I was going to resolve this whole thing with Publius and the curse of too much vision, so he was just going to lie in his vault screaming for the next however many of these there are going to be! Hamilton here: Jay I don't want you to write any more of these. Madison, please take these numbers.

Federalist 55: The Total Number of the House of Representatives. Publius realizes it was all a dream.

Federalist 56: The Same Subject Continued. Publius reunites with Bill for a classic adventure!

Federalist 57: The Alleged Tendency of the Plan to Elevate the Few at the Expense of the Many Considered in Connection with Representation. The Articles of Confederation burn down an innocent village.

Federalist 58: Objection That the Number of Members Will Not Be Augmented as the Progress of Population Demands Considered. Bill and Publius locate the Articles of Confederation's secret hideout.

Federalist 59: Concerning the Power of Congress to Regulate the Election of Members. Publius and Bill assemble a crack team from all thirteen former British colonies to march on the Articles of Confederation together and take America back!

Federalist 60: The Same Subject Continued. Recruitment montage.

Federalist 61: The Same Subject Continued. Training montage.

Federalist 62: The Senate. Publius and his team make a daring assault on the Articles of Confederation's hideaway.

Federalist 63: The Senate Continued. It's a trap! Publius and the team are surrounded.

Federalist 64: The Powers of the Senate. Bill of Rights volunteers to sacrifice himself to hold them off while Publius escapes.

Federalist 65: The Powers of the Senate Continued. Publius swears he will come back for him, if that is what a majority of the states want.

Federalist 66: Objections to the Power of the Senate to Sit as a Court for Impeachments Further Considered. Bill dies heroically as Publius makes his way into the control room of the Articles of Confederation, where a surprise awaits him.

Federalist 67: The Executive Department. The Articles of Confederation are Publius's father!

Federalist 68: The Mode of Electing the President. Publius screams and screams.

Federalist 69: The Real Character of the Executive. Publius is torn. Can he destroy the Articles of Confederation? What, after all this time, is he fighting for?

Federalist 70: The Executive Department Further Considered. Publius hears a familiar voice.

Federalist 71: The Duration in Office of the Executive. It's Socrates, his old mentor!

Federalist 72: The Same Subject Continued, and Re-Eligibility of the Executive Considered. Socrates tells Publius that he believes in him and knows he'll find a way to do what is best for the people.

Federalist 73: The Provision for Support of the Executive, and the Veto Power. Publius and the Articles of Confederation fight dramatically.

Federalist 74: The Command of the Military and Naval Forces, and the Pardoning Power of the Executive. Due to its limited powers and lack of energy and direction, the Articles of Confederation cannot withstand Publius. Publius fights the Articles of Confederation back to the edge of a New Hampshire cliff.

Federalist 75: The Treaty-Making Power of the Executive. The Articles of Confederation dangle off the edge of the cliff.

Federalist 76: The Appointing Power of the Executive. "Please, Publius," the Articles of Confederation beg. Publius grabs the hand of the Articles of Confederation.

Federalist 77: The Appointing Power Continued and Other Powers of the Executive Considered. The wily Articles of Confederation pull Publius down with them.

Federalist 78: The Judiciary Department. Publius falls through the air with the Articles of Confederation.

Federalist 79: The Judiciary Continued. Publius screams and screams.

Federalist 80: The Powers of the Judiciary. Publius is about to hit the earth when . . . something stops him.

Federalist 81: The Judiciary Continued, and the Distribution of Judicial Authority. It's the cat! The cat he saved from a tree in Federalist 1. It's much bigger now.

Federalist 82: The Judiciary Continued. Publius kisses the cat passionately, and the cat turns into the beautiful woman from Federalist 19, which Publius of course always knew would happen and wasn't surprised by at all.

Federalist 83: The Judiciary Continued in Relation to Trial by Jury. We check in again with Publius's roommates.

Federalist 84: Certain General and Miscellaneous Objections to the Constitution Considered and Answered. Publius answers and considers certain general and miscellaneous objections to the Constitution.

Federalist 85: Concluding Remarks. Big wedding!

The Composing of
"To Anacreon in Heaven,"
c. 1778

The National Anthem is set to the same tune as "To Anacreon in Heaven"!

Don't you think this last phrase is a little high?
Who cares? Amos, this is a drinking song.
No, I know. I just worry about that one note.
Don't! This is not a song that needs to sound good when lots and lots of people sing it. This is not for elementary schools and sporting events. This is a song for drunk people to sing.
I'm just saying it's very high.
But that's like the joke of it, though, is that it suddenly jumps up a full octave and everyone singing it is going to be super drunk, and it's going to sound hilarious.
Yeah, but I mean we want it to be singable.
I honestly don't think that needs to be a priority. Would it sound better if the people who sang it could hit the note? Sure. But nobody is going to be *required* to sing this song. People who cannot hit the weird high note can simply decide not to sing it, and nobody will be bothered by that decision. No one is going to go around to gatherings of people and say, "No, before you do your thing, you've got to sing 'To Anacreon in Heaven' first."
I guess not.
I know not. That is not an eventuality we need to plan for.

But it wouldn't be bad if it were more singable.

I just don't think we need to worry about this. This is a drinking song. It doesn't need to be, like, "God Save the King." It's only ever going to be a drinking song. It's just an unsingable drinking song, and that's totally fine.

You admit it is unsingable!

Only that one part, though, which, again, I don't see being a huge issue. Nobody listens to drinking songs and thinks, wow, that's an exquisite melody, and if we ever needed to replace "God Save the King" suddenly, that would be the tune I would use. Nothing is going to happen to "God Save the King."

"God Save the King" is very singable.

It is. It's a classic. This doesn't need to be that. But it's like, what do you think is going to happen? The thirteen colonies that currently comprise British possessions in North America are going to secede because there was an unexpected tax on all their paper goods and they felt like they should have gotten more input on it, and then their untrained ragtag militias will manage to defeat the greatest army in the world and they will start a new country, which will then find itself at war again about thirty years later, but involving British Canada this time, and somebody watching a battle near Baltimore, Maryland, specifically, will be looking to see if the new American flag is there, and when he sees the flag, he will write a long poem about it that also includes some verses insulting the opposing forces that will become more and more of a problem as time passes, and the poem will be set to this specific tune, and people will be forced to sing it at public gatherings for the next two hundred years including sporting events and will slowly come to the realization as a nation that it is completely unsingable, and they will start thinking of it as a kind of symbolic, almost, failure, that their nation's anthem contains a note just a little too high for everyone to hit, and maybe that's representative, and they will think, maybe this hollowness has always been at the heart of this country, maybe this country's highest promise has always been synonymous with heartbreak, and it will all be our fault, because we didn't foresee that specific scenario when we wrote this drinking song?

No.

Right, well, exactly.

Seneca Falls for You

Did you know that the Seneca Falls conference on the rights of women in July 1848, featuring Lucretia Mott and Elizabeth Cady Stanton, almost didn't happen, because whenever a work-oriented woman goes to a small town for any reason, the town tries to seize her and put her into a Hallmark romance? More people should teach about that.

The town clock of Seneca Falls struck six.

Drat. Elizabeth Cady S. sighed. She shrugged back her long tresses, the color of a mottled brown river. A river after a heavy rain, or possibly a river downstream from a farm. It was so late, already. She would have to go over her Declaration of Sentiments by candlelight. She clambered up the steps to the local accommodation.

"Can I help you?"

Elizabeth looked up. And there he was. He was wearing a shirt that was open at the collar, and she could see his sunburned throat and a provocative, sensual hat that taunted her with what it concealed. Probably a forehead, but you could never be sure.

He took a deep, masculine inhale. She blushed fiercely.

"What brings you to town?" he inquired.

"I'm here," she said, in a voice that quavered like a baby bird might if it were cupped in strong masculine hands that were incorrectly placing it back into a tree after finding it on the ground, rather than waiting for its parent bird to come along, "for the convention."

He looked puzzled. "The convention?" he inquired.

"On the rights of women," Elizabeth said.

"Women," he said. He looked off into the distance in a manner that was steely yet haunted, like a railway trestle full of ghosts.

"Ye-es," said Elizabeth. "A lot of us are in town for that."

"I knew a woman once," he said. His shirt flapped somberly open, revealing more of his chest. Suddenly she was aware of small footsteps approaching from the southeast. For a woman, she excelled at cardinal directions. She glanced over and saw a small boy, who looked like a neat little tintype of the man in the shirt. "This is our son Timmy. She gave birth to him before she—"

"Oh," Elizabeth said. "I'm sorry."

"It was a long time ago," the man said.

"He looks seven," Elizabeth said.

"It was seven years ago," he said. "I'm Christopher. I run this little inn. Seneca Falls is my home. I hope you'll come to love Seneca Falls just as much as I do."

"Well," Elizabeth said, "I'm not staying. I'm just in town for the convention." She swallowed. "We are trying to make certain that women have rights. Maybe even voting rights. Specifically white women, though."

Christopher nodded, but in a way that did not look as though he were listening very closely. "Sorry," he said. "I was lost in your eyes."

"Oh," Elizabeth said. "I hope you managed to find your way out of my eyes."

Christopher shook his head rapidly, like a wet dog. "I may never," he said.

Timmy cooed appreciatively. "My sensitive single dad is in love with you," he said, "and you are going to stay in Seneca Falls and be my new mommy."

"Whoa there!" Christopher said. "Don't get ahead of yourself, Timmy!" He rumpled Timmy's flaxen hair. Timmy looked up with his wide, innocent blue eyes. "But I hope you'll make time to come to the baking contest."

"Baking contest?" Elizabeth asked.

"Oh yes," Christopher said. "It's a Seneca Falls tradition. You're going to love it here. Would you like to go ice skating right now?"

"Ice skating?" Elizabeth asked. "But it's . . . the summer."

Christopher winked. "Seneca Falls is a pretty special place." He leaned in conspiratorially. "We have a gazebo."

≈

Elizabeth sat on her bed trying to work on the Declaration of Sentiments. *We hold these truths to be self-evident*, she wrote. She sighed. *That all men and women are created . . .* It was hard to concentrate. There was an absolutely marvelous aroma drifting up from the kitchen. Finally she blew out her candle, set the Declaration down, and went downstairs in the direction of the scent.

"What is that wonderful smell?"

"Oh!" A gray-haired woman in an apron looked up from where she was rolling out dough. "What perfect timing! I was just baking cookies!"

"For the baking contest?" Elizabeth asked.

"Just for the love of it," the woman said. She smiled. "I'm Christopher's mother, Timmy's grandmother. Would you like to join me?"

"I've got to work on the Declaration of Sentiments," Elizabeth said. "I have just gotten to the part where men and women are created equal."

The woman sighed indulgently. "You city girls are all hustle and bustle!"

"I just wanted to see what smelled so good," Elizabeth said, "but I can't stop here. This may be a key step on the road to women's suffrage!"

The woman sighed a second time. "In my day," she said, "we didn't have suffrage, or property rights."

"We still don't have those things," Elizabeth said, "in the overwhelming majority of states and territories."

"But we had something more precious than that. Family. And a place to belong." She beamed brilliantly, like a goose that had been set on fire.

"Thank you," Elizabeth said uncertainly.

"Well, go work on your declaration!" the woman said. "But if you change your mind, there's an apron with your name on it. There will always be a place for you in this kitchen."

"How did you know my name?" Elizabeth asked. "Did you read the fliers advertising the convention?"

"You just looked like an Elizabeth." The woman smiled and held the apron out. It smelled so good in the kitchen, and upstairs suddenly seemed very far.

"Maybe just a batch," Elizabeth said. She put the apron on.

≈

"Can I lick the spoon?" Timmy asked.

Elizabeth hoisted him up to the counter so that he could. It felt so natural and important to be lifting up this young boy. She wondered how she had spent so much of her life lifting herself up and lifting up women like herself, when she could have been lifting up small boys.

"My, my," Christopher said. "It's my two favorite girls!"

Elizabeth spun around, accidentally spraying him with flour. He chuckled a warm, masculine chuckle and flicked some of it back at her. Timmy clapped his hands.

"It smells wonderful in here," Christopher said. "Has somebody been baking?" He took a big bite of a gingerbread woman. "Wow."

"Elizabeth created all these gingerbread men and women," his mother said. "They're all created equal—ly delicious."

The words seemed somehow familiar. Elizabeth wasn't sure how. They were like the echo of something long, long ago.

"I think Elizabeth has finally discovered that she belongs in the kitchen," Christopher's mother continued, with a broad, supportive beam, like something that was load-bearing for a building.

Elizabeth blushed. "It's nothing," she said. She dusted her hands off on her apron, then removed it, folded it, and began to head upstairs.

"Would you look at that?" Christopher said. He was on the stairs behind her, pointing up. "Mistletoe."

≈

Elizabeth flung herself back onto her bed. Her brain reeled, like a style of dance that was not unpopular in the time period. She had kissed Christopher! And Christopher had kissed her back! In her busy life in the city, she never had time for this sort of thing. She really ought to work on the Declaration of Sentiments. But for the first time in her life, she was feeling sentiments rather than just declaring them. What a wonderful place Seneca Falls was! It could be a home! Wasn't that just the place a woman belonged, a home?

≈

"Lizzie?" Lucretia Mott inquired. "Where has thee been?"

"I was just thinking," Elizabeth said. "All this talk about sentiments, but what are we really *feeling*?"

Lucretia turned pale. "Lizzie?"

"We work so hard for individual property rights and suffrage," Elizabeth said. "But what if all we needed, all along, was love?"

"Lizzie," Lucretia said, "thee will make us ridiculous."

"Maybe we were ridiculous before," Elizabeth said. "Maybe, now, for the first time, we're actually making sense. For the first time in my life, I'm feeling sentiments rather than just declaring them."

Lucretia furrowed her brow in a way men had often told her was unappealing. "Lizzie," she said, "thee has a husband at home and has for many years."

Elizabeth blinked at her. "Seneca Falls is my home," she said. "I have a life here with Christopher." The clock struck three. "Now, if you'll excuse me, I'm going to be late for the baking contest."

"Lizzie!" Lucretia cried, with growing dread. "It is as I feared. It is as I warned against. Thee stayed in the town. And now Seneca Falls has thee. Was it a picturesque lodging house?"

Elizabeth shrugged. "Yes," she said. "Why?"

Lucretia groaned. "Then we are lost." She seized the Declaration of Sentiments from Elizabeth's hands and pored over it, her eyes growing wide with terror.

Lizzie <3 Christopher. Lizzie <3 Christopher. Lizzie <3 Christopher. Lizzie <3 Christopher.

Lucretia shuddered and let it fall from her hands. "It was a mistake to choose Seneca Falls for this conference, and I have paid the price. Get out, all of you, while you still can!"

"Get out?" Elizabeth asked, blinking curiously, like a doll. "But why? I think Seneca Falls is ever so nice. I think I'd like to stay here forever."

50 States of Grey

God, he wanted it so badly. He could not sleep from wanting it. He tossed and turned. The sheet slipped slowly lower and lower, like the Mason Dixon. The room was very hot, and it was shaped like a square, not like an oval. Maybe he would never get to be in the room shaped like an oval.

He imagined being there—caressing its smooth sides. Henry Clay clenched his fists.

He would probably never be president.

Excerpt from
Modern Etiquette
(1793 edition)

A fascinating thing about the past is that there is almost no limit to the determination of your textbooks to see historical correspondence as platonic! And I found out why: they understood that all correspondence was composed in accordance with this guide. Sure, the result sounds pretty passionate, but that was just the style at the time. They were trying to obey a strict formula that follows below.

On Writing Platonic Letters

In these modern times one is often compelled to convey thoughts and messages to a variety of individuals, many of whom are not your spouse . . . or even a member of the fairer sex! Are you seeking to communicate with someone? Here is a guide, young letter writer! Write confidently!

_____ _____:
             A.   *B.*

I _____ for the _____ of your
          C.   *D.*

_____ . How my _____
        E.   *F.*

_____ _____when
        G.   *H.*

I contemplated your last _____for the
                           I.

_____th time, pressing it to my _____
  J.   *K.*

and inhaling _____ lungfuls of your
               L.

_____ scent. I hope that all is well in
        M.

_____ and that the
          N.

_____ is tolerable. You _____
      O.   *P.*

A. (Superlative Adjective Expressing the Maximum Amount of Affection You Can Have for Somebody)

B. (Friend's Name)

C. (verb that describes a starving man's attitude toward food)

D. (noun, your favorite sense)

E. (noun, body part)

F. (adjective that describes a baby bird)

G. (noun, the most intimate part of yourself)

H. (past-tense verb, another way of saying "throbbed")

I. (noun, word that means "letter" but fancy)

J. (worryingly high number)

K. (noun, body part)

L. (adjective, how you'd describe a whale)

M. (adjective, the way you would describe a gift from God Almighty)

N. (Proper Noun, place at least three days distant by train)

O. (noun, something that takes years and might kill you)

P. (verb, what a deer does)

through my dreams, carrying my _____

                                        Q.

in your hand. _____Without you I am a(n) _____

                    R.   *S.*

_____; I feel but a _____

            T.   *U.*

_____ in your absence.

            V.

When I next see you, I shall cover your _____with

                                                    W.

_____, _____

            X.   *Y.*

_____ .

            Z.

Your fiancé(e) sends (his/her) best also.

With a thousand _____, your platonic friend,

                    aa.

_____

            bb.

Q. (noun, internal organ without which life would be considerably more difficult)

R. (Ejaculation!)

S. (adjective, how a jack-o'-lantern is on November 1)

T. (noun, something that haunts)

U. (adjective, describing a sickly Victorian boy)

V. (noun, thing you find in an attic)

W. (noun, body part)

X. (adjective, how the Mariana Trench is)

Y. (adjective, how a shipwrecked sailor feels)

Z. (plural noun, something a dog bestows)

aa. (plural noun, intimate acts)

bb. (Your Name)

A Speech in Favor of Constructing the Eerie Canal That Got Pretty Far Along Before the Speaker Realized Erie Starts with Only One E

New York definitely built a canal in the early nineteenth century that was a thrilling engineering triumph and rocked the world of transporting goods from one place to another in a big way, at least until the railroad came along. Before that happened, though, the state had to approve its construction. This is some pro-canal oratory that I can only assume that the orator tried very hard to suppress.

Fellow New Yorkers, it is very good to see such enthusiasm for an idea of such excellence. Yes, it is beyond time that we built an Eerie Canal! What could be better than such an addition to our state?

When we look around in this year 1817 and see the numerous other states, full of scary turnpikes, frightening macadam roads, and terror-ridden causeways, we may well say to ourselves, why have we nothing to match them? Where is our haunting, spectral waterway? Why have we no canal that goes bump in the night? Where, in short, is New York's eerie canal?

Ours is a time full of monstrosities: lorgnettes, antimacassars, the Fulton steamboat.

Well, if this be a time of monstrosity, should New York not have the best? We must have a grand and terrifying canal, a canal full of ghosts and goblins, a canal that freezes the blood in the veins and makes the teeth chatter. A canal that is riddled with ominous songs about decapitation. Low bridge! Everybody down! Everybody down, or I cannot answer for your fate!

WHY SHOULD OUR STATE LACK HAUNTING, SPECTRAL VISIONS SUCH AS THOSE OF WHICH RHODE ISLAND BOASTS? Why should other states such as South Carolina, nay, or Virginia, even humble Vermont, possess canals that pulsate with an ominous, indefinable energy, that chill the blood of all who behold them, and New York shall have none? New York is a state as spooky as any in the union. Aaron Burr has made this state his home.

"Never shake thy gory locks at me," cries Macbeth, in the eponymous play *Macbeth*. I love Shakespeare, and I know that at that moment, Macbeth is addressing a ghost, but when our canal has completed its construction, he may as well be addressing our canal! Our canal will be not *an* eerie canal but *the* eerie canal. It will be unmistakably haunting, full of fogs and wails; it will be atmospheric and discomfiting! Its locks will be the goriest of all! Not all the people who ship their scary goods on it from terrifying Waterford to spooky New York City will be confident of return!

Massachusetts has its witch hunts and the city of Boston. New Hampshire has something big that goes *screeeee*. Florida is not yet a state, just a frightening idea! Maybe, on our eerie canal, people can whisper about what it would be like if Florida were real.

New York was originally one of America's leading spooky states, as we can see from these charts.

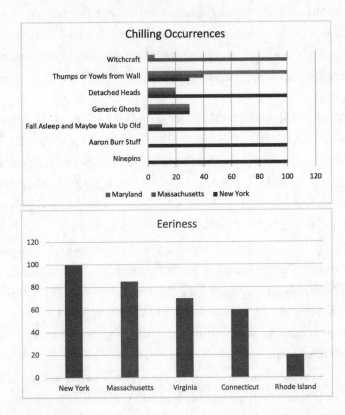

When people played at ninepins in the mountains with Dutch ghosts, they did it here! When headless horsemen were looking for places they could settle and unsettle others, they were headless right here in the Empire State. But since those days, our spookiness levels have gone way, way down, and the spookiness levels of other places have gone way, way up! Edgar Allan Poe is growing up in Baltimore right now, and things there are getting eerier by the minute.

Thank heavens for this canal! We must make it so scary that people will be unwilling to transport anything along it and will depend instead upon the railroad for all their commerce! We must spare no—what?

. . . ah, I see.

Where's Walden?

I don't know why Henry David Thoreau's children's book was never published.

Can you find the following?
Look everywhere on this page for:

+ a man seated on a pumpkin who is happy
+ a man on a velvet cushion who is crowded and UNHAPPY
+ enough bricks and wood to make a snug house to keep out the cold, which any man may have who knows to look for them
+ a man who does not know he has wealth enough
+ your ma coming with the laundry so that you can live in perfect independence and solitude*
+ one man who truly knows himself
+ a drummer drumming somewhat distantly
+ a drummer drumming but a little bit nearer
+ your own drummer whose beat you must follow however measured or far away
+ me but with a mustache instead of just a neck beard
+ my nearest neighbor
+ a mass of men living lives of quiet desperation
+ a foolish consistency, the hobgoblin of small minds
+ Walden Pond
+ my friend Ralph Waldo Emerson

* True!

Emily Dickinson Content!!!

Emily "The Belle of Amherst" Dickinson was here to do two things: have a super distinctive writing style and avoid human interaction! Here is some Emily Dickinson content!

Emily Dickinson Chats with Tech Support

DEREK: Hi there! Thank you so much for contacting customer support, Emily! How can I help?

EMILY: I Cannot Write In Sentence Case
I Look—to You—for Aid
And If—I Rest—My Hands
Upon the Keys—A Dash is Made

I do not Mean—to Write
Like This—It is no Proper Hand
Why it Inserts—such Dashes
I Cannot Understand

I Wish—to write Words—Normally

DEREK: Hey Emily! I'm so sorry for the keyboard issue. It sounds like a hardware problem.

EMILY: Dear Thomas Wentworth Higginson
   Says—I Have Got—A Style
   But I don't Mean to Have A—Style
   I need my—Keyboard Fixed

DEREK: I'm going to need you to turn your machine off and on again.

EMILY: Having it Once Turned Off
   Can I—Be Sure—It Will Return?
   I fear Much to Dispatch It to
   That Undiscover'd Bourne

DEREK: This is just a standard thing we tell everyone to do with their machines and should not be a problem, Emily!

EMILY: I shall Attempt—
   To Dispatch It—
   Into this Silent Realm
   Beyond where—Mousy Tooth may Gnaw
   Or Rust and Moth Consume

DEREK: Emily, have you restarted your machine?

EMILY: I have Emerged from Joysome—Death

DEREK: So it seems like you're still having the issue, huh?

EMILY: No—That Time Was—A Stylistic—Choice
   Oh No—I Am Still Having—The Problem

Emily Dickinson Plays Taboo

It is a bee.
. . . is it a bee? Just FYI in case I didn't explain the rules correctly,
you can't say the thing that it is.

It has a song.
A bird?
It has a sting—
A hornet?
Ah, too, it has a wing.
Are you 100 percent that it isn't a bee?
Wasp?
Mean bat?
It was fame.
Emily how are we supposed to get fame from this?

The thing with feathers
An owl
That perches in the soul
An owl?
Never asks for a crumb
An owl who isn't very hungry
It sings the tune without the words
I'm going to keep guessing owl until you indicate otherwise
I've heard it in the hilliest land and on the strangest sea
A well-traveled owl
Hope!
Emily.

A fine invention
The steam engine.
For Gentlemen who see!
A magnifying glass.
Glasses.
A microscope is better
A telescope?
Faith.
Emily!

Solemnest of industries enacted upon earth.
Mining? Copper mining? Meatpacking?
Wheelwrighting?
The sweeping up the Heart
Meatpacking!!!
And putting love away
Wait, I'm confused, it's an industry, though? Is it Greeting Cards?
What was it.
The Bustle in a House the Morning after Death.
That's not an industry, Emily.

It was not Death, for I stood up
Okay, so not death
It was not Night
Emily, this isn't good
It was not Frost
Um, a sunny afternoon?
Nor fire
Emily, I need more here

And yet it tasted like them all
. . . I'm lost here I have to say
Psilocybin?

A narrow Fellow in the Grass
Snake
Yes!
Oh my God!!!

Emily Dickinson Goes on *Family Feud*

Fast Money portion!

Name something that follows the word Pork. **Bellied Gust**

Name a country a man with a mustache should visit to meet a woman with a mustache. **That Sublime Inlet of the Soul**

Name something that's hard to do with your eyes open. **Dwell in Time**

Name somebody a man might not want to tell that he uses Viagra. **A Narrow Fellow in the Grass**

A traffic sign that best describes your love life. **Come Slowly, Eden**

Name something that a person with long legs might not be able to fit into. **The Carriage with Horses' Heads Pointed Toward Immortality**

Tell me something that a pilot might turn on after the plane takes off. **Expectancy**

I could never make love to someone who looked like who. **A Man**

What's the first question somebody asks when they wake up from a coma? **Who are you?**

Another way people say "Mother" **Still Nature's Bosom**

Something you buy in bulk **Fascicles**

A word that rhymes with frog **Bog**

On a scale from 1 to 10 how likely are you to live to 100 **0***

* She actually scored 50 points!

Edgar Allan Poe's Handyman

Edgar Allan Poe lived in Baltimore and was one of the fathers of Gothic horror and mystery fiction! He also wrote a long poem about bells. A fascinating guy!

One thing people don't know about Edgar Allan Poe is that in each of the early drafts of his classic works, he wrote a scene where a handyman comes in and tries to address the problem at the center of the plot.

The Black Cat

"Oh, I see the problem here. You have bricked the cat inside the wall. That is why your wall is making a noise. You see, I tap it here, and it goes, 'Meow.' That isn't a wall sound. That's a cat sound. Yeah, I can get it out, but I will have to drill into the drywall."

The Cask of Amontillado

"Yes, I see the problem here. Whoever built this wall here in the wine area didn't leave an egress, and there is a guy stuck inside here."

The Tell-Tale Heart

"No, I'm listening to the floor, and I don't hear the horrid beating of a hideous heart. Or the beating of a heart of any kind. I can double-check for you, but I'm going to have to break open the floor, and that'll be a whole operation. You sure it's bugging you?"

The Raven

"I see your problem. You left the door open, and a bird got in."

The Fall of the House of Usher

"Yes, there is definitely something the matter with this house. Not metaphorically. There is a barely perceptible fissure that runs in a zigzag all the way down the front of the house until it becomes lost in the waters of the tarn. That is a serious structural problem for this home, especially because the masonry is in such bad shape. This is going to be a very expensive renovation, frankly, and I think I would relocate. All you need is one bolt of lightning, and boom, your house splits in half and sinks into the tarn."

The Masque of the Red Death

"I see your problem. This whole back room is full of plague. This is a very badly designed party space."

The Pit and the Pendulum

"I see your problem here. You have put the pit right under the pendulum. That is not a good location for either of those things. This is a very dangerous room."

───────────── ★ ─────────────

Herman Melville
Pitches His Editor

*Herman "I Love Boats and Nathaniel Hawthorne" Melville is
best known today for writing* Moby-Dick, *a book about whales
and boats. But he also wrote a book called* Pierre, or the Ambi-
guities, *that is a pretty wild ride! This piece is not about that,
however.*

Okay, it's a book about whales.
Go on.
That's it, just whales.
Are you a whale expert?
**Kind of? I mean I know a lot of facts about whales, defi-
nitely, but none of them are correct.**
Herman, that doesn't sound like you're a whale expert. Thought:
what if it weren't entirely about whales? What if it were also
about other things?
**Okay, but I must have the whale parts. Here is what I think
would be a good ratio. Half of it will be a novel, and the
other half will just be me telling my favorite facts about
whales. How does that sound?**
So it's two books?
No, it is one book inside the other book.
So half of the book is an action book, and then it becomes a
whale book, and then it returns to the plot.

No, I was thinking more like, every chapter. Like there'll be one chapter about the plot, and then there will be a chapter where I talk about sperm for ten pages and none of the facts are correct.

Huh.

I expect it will be widely regarded as a classic of Western literature.

—

My next book is about a man who just sits there.

And—

And nothing. He just sits there.

Ah.

His name is Bartleby.

That's great.

He's a scrivener.

Ah.

He scrivens.

Okay.

Except he doesn't want to scriven that day.

So he says "I'd prefer not to."

Who put you in touch with me?

The Scarlet Letter,
Abridged

Noted Bowdoin hottie Nathaniel Hawthorne published this book in 1850, even though it is set in Puritan times. I have always hated this book.

Hester Prynne walks out of jail.

TOWNSPEOPLE: Shame!
HESTER PRYNNE: Please, everyone, my eyes are up here.
    Although I guess the scarlet letter that marks my infamy is down there.

REV DIMMESDALE: Hey Hester
    Very embarrassing that you have this baby
    For you I mean
    And nobody else
    Because obviously no one else could have been involved
HESTER: Yup, that's how babies are made.
DIMMESDALE: I'm so glad you agree.

HESTER: Husband I see you are back now
    Very sorry about . . . all this
CHILLINGWORTH: Shhh please don't acknowledge me
    I'm doing a new thing where I'm not your husband
    Also I want everyone to call me Roger

HESTER: Roger

CHILLINGWORTH: Roger Chillingworth

HESTER: I can't tell if you're making this up on the spot

CHILLINGWORTH: My name is Roger Chillingworth now and I have a detailed backstory

HESTER: Is this even related to, you know, my thing?

CHILLINGWORTH: Do you want to hear my detailed backstory

Hester sighs

CHILLINGWORTH: Things are so much more fun and spooky now!

Please don't acknowledge me though unless you want to be like, love that guy's name,

Never met him though

PEARL: Mother what does the letter on your chest mean?

HESTER: It's an A I got for doing adultery.

PEARL: You must be very good at adultery.

Hester sighs

DIMMESDALE: Wow Roger Chillingworth! Good to meet you! Cool name by the way

CHILLINGWORTH: Thanks it's my real name that I was born with

DIMMESDALE: Anyway so embarrassing about Hester Prynne and how she had that shameful baby totally unassisted

CHILLINGWORTH: Yeah that was random

DIMMESDALE: Totally random

I don't think it even looks like me at all! But obviously it's a well-known fact about babies that they can look any way they want so if it did look like me it wouldn't be weird or suspicious.

CHILLINGWORTH: No

CHILLINGWORTH: Do you want to come live in my house for no reason

JUDGE: We are going to take your baby away

HESTER: Honestly please go for it she's starting to creep me out

Pearl starts to scream; a hideous wind rises and everyone's wigs fly off

JUDGE: On second thought you can keep the baby

HESTER: Nooo

CHILLINGWORTH: Hey roomie

DIMMESDALE: Um

CHILLINGWORTH: What if I gave you a free tattoo

DIMMESDALE: Is this a situation where I can say no?

CHILLINGWORTH: I don't know. Are you the father of Hester Prynne's child?

HESTER: Reverend Dimmesdale, you don't look so good

DIMMESDALE: (shivering and sweating) I'm totally fine
You look good though

Pearl goes skipping through the house, and every item in it levitates ominously

HESTER: Are you 100% that nobody is going to take Pearl
    I am definitely an unfit mother

DIMMESDALE: No you definitely get to keep her

HESTER: Oh good that is the outcome I wanted

DIMMESDALE: (whispering) Do you think our sins are forgiven

CHILLINGWORTH: What was that

HESTER: Hi, "Roger Chillingworth"

CHILLINGWORTH: I hear you doing air quotes and it's hurtful

DIMMESDALE: Hey everyone in the community I am definitely dying

But before I go I want to be sure that everyone sees the cool free tattoo that I got from my friend and roommate, Roger Chillingworth

I think it's going to answer a lot of questions you may or may not have had

TOWNSPEOPLE: Is it an A?

DIMMESDALE: No one knows what it is

It's a *complete mystery*

TOWNSPEOPLE: it's definitely an A

Dimmesdale dramatically rips off his shirt

TOWNSPEOPLE: Reverend Dimmesdale is showing the community his big A that he got for doing adultery

DIMMESDALE: (dying) I just thought everyone would be more surprised

50 States of Grey

"That's it!" he said. "I give up! It's unfindable!"

He sank down and sighed heavily. He had been fumbling around this watery body, greeted by nothing but iciness and chill, and the occasional unpleasantly tight icy grip that threatened to snap his vessel in half at the waist. They kept telling him it was there, that he would find it, and that once he found it, it would bring pleasure and profit to them both. But it was a myth.

He was not going to find the Northwest Passage.

Moby-Dick:
An Oral History

You thought you were done hearing about Herman Melville, but you weren't. Sorry. Here is more.

ISHMAEL: Call me Ishmael.

QUEEQUEG: His name is not Ishmael. But I'm always like, call people what they want to be called.

STARBUCK: The voyage was not my idea.

AHAB: The voyage was a great idea.

QUEEQUEG: Let me put it this way: it was the kind of voyage where midway through you start building yourself a coffin.

ISHMAEL: I thought it was overdramatic that Queequeg started literally building himself a coffin. It was very emo and passive aggressive, I thought.

AHAB: Ultimately we tried to tell people it was a very small lifeboat with a lid, but it was definitely a coffin.

QUEEQUEG: It was not a very small boat with a lid. It was a coffin, because I wanted people to understand all that I was feeling.

ISHMAEL: In fact, I found all the coffin allusions extremely heavy-handed.

AHAB: The first leg of the voyage went fine. That's all you need, really. A good first leg.

STARBUCK: The voyage was extremely stressful.

GOLD PIECE: I got nailed to the mast.

STARBUCK: Everyone kept telling us whale facts, and *none of them were correct.*

ISHMAEL: I think some of the whale facts were correct.

FLASK: The whale facts were all bogus.

QUEEQUEG: It was very frustrating because we would be moving along and meeting ships and crossing a lot of ocean, and then suddenly we would have to stop and hear inaccurate facts about whales for a long time.

ISHMAEL: They were fun facts. I liked hearing about the whales.

PIP THE CABIN BOY: I liked the whale facts better than when we reenacted *King Lear.*

QUEEQUEG: Oh, yeah, we did reenact *King Lear.* (pensively twirls a shrunken human head around his finger) This was a weird trip.

AHAB: The takeaway from *King Lear* is that King Lear did nothing wrong.

STARBUCK: There came a point when we were around the equator and we had lost all our navigational equipment and really should not still have been out there, but of course that was when we saw the whale.

AHAB: The timing was perfect! One more day, and we would have lost that monster.

MOBY DICK: I'm glad you reached out to me for this story. I would very much like to be excluded from this narrative. I think previous accounts have made it seem as though I wanted any part of this, or as if I were some kind of supernatural inspirational force, or even an active participant who realized what a big impact I had made on this guy's life but— how do I put this—

AHAB: Moby Dick was the one fixation of my life. I eat Moby Dick, breathe Moby Dick, live Moby Dick, spit my last breath at Moby Dick from Hell's heart.

MOBY DICK: I can barely keep track of how many guys blame me for their lost legs.

AHAB: We are a pair locked in mythical combat. Only one can prevail. We are two sides of a coin, like the coin nailed to the mast.

MOBY DICK: It's a lot.

AHAB: Moby Dick is my other half, literally in the sense that Moby Dick has half of my legs and metaphorically too.

MOBY DICK: I genuinely could not pick the guy out of a lineup, but I did charge at the boat because charging recklessly at boats is my one passion.

AHAB: Moby Dick recognized me immediately and resumed our epic conflict.

MOBY DICK: I think it's more about him than it is about me. Although I am sorry about his leg. And the boat. All the boats.

QUEEQUEG: As it turned out, I was right to make the coffin.

ISHMAEL: I just hate it when someone does something as dramatic as building a coffin for themselves and then it turns out they are RIGHT to have done so, and it literally saves your life.

STARBUCK: It was a terrible voyage. The good news is that my legacy is so scant, I will never see my name or likeness used to advertise a mediocre product.

AHAB: I would rate the voyage as mostly a success.

---★---

Songs Not of Myself, by Walt Whitman

You've tolerated his Leaves of Grass. *You've delighted in his* Songs of Myself. *Now it's time for you to bask in . . . treasured American poet Walt Whitman's* Songs of Other People. *If CDs had been invented, these covers would be on a number of CDs, but instead he will come to your house and intone them in a bardly manner until you can get him to stop. He contains multitudes, apparently!*

My Milkshake
Come to the yard, boys!
I have made a milkshake
I have made a milkshake for you
It is the best of the milkshakes
I say it, I swear it
It is better than yours, and all the rest
I would teach you, but it would be costly
Too rich by far, such knowledge

Barbie Girl
Barbie, I salute you!
Ken, I return your salutation!

In my vehicle, four-wheeled, purring above the open road, will
    you ride beside me?
Allons-y, Ken!
Jump in, then, Barbie! Jump in, my camarado!

I am a Barbie, eternal, feminine
I celebrate myself and sing myself
For this is a world of Barbies and I am in it
Content in my life, in my hair, glistening, and its plenteous
    combs
I will go to the bank by the woods and become undisguised
    and naked
I will go anywhere; I am unashamed
I am Barbie, I contain multitudes
What your imagination contains, I contain

Make me walk, make me talk, do whatever you please
I can act like a star, for I am a star
I can beg on my knees, for there is no shame in begging
There is nothing shameful in my body
I am Barbie, I am yours
You can touch, for I write first the poetry of the body, of its
    plastic
Of its feet, tiny, not load-bearing, ankles, calves, knees
    bendless, hips rotary, the blank flat expanse between hips
    and hair, the firm orbic sisters, the lustrous bounty of
    coiffure
Plastic, skin-shelled, glistening from the lathe, I am fantastical
I embrace my bounteous life!
I love you, Ken!

All-Star

Somebody out of the crowd said to me,

O Beware the world! Beware the rolling world!

There are many tools in the shed, the hammer, the adze, the
awl, the saw, the lathe, the trowel, the shovel, the pick, the
pickax, the hoe, many the tools of the laborer, varying one
from another in their sharpness.

Beware! For you are not one of the sharpest, the well-honed
ax, nor the adze, nor the sharp-edged saw

I remember how she stood there, and said this to me, with her
hand lifted to her brow in the sign of an L

The years start, coming, onrushing, unceasing, never
stopping

I hit the ground, running, ineluctably

I see no reason to live for anything but pleasure

I see the man with his mighty brain, toiling and laboring,
while his sinews languish

But I, I take to the back streets

I make no apology: I have done no wrong

Come! Let us take to the back roads

We will never know if we do not venture

We will never shine if we are not first effulgent

Come! You are a star!

I tell you: everything that glitters is golden

I tell you: you are a meteor, transcendent, crucible-breaking.

YMCA

What are you doing young man?
Are you so morose, so given up to these ostensible realities,
    politics, points, your ambition or whatever it may be?
Are you dismayed? There is no need to be dismayed, though
    you are in a new town
I, I am not new
I see you and look to embrace you

Therefore young man,
From the ground of the cobbled cities,
From the ground, kissed by the dust of travelers,
The ground, trod by the hirsute bull, the buffalo
Pick up yourself, young man!
There is no need to be unhappy.
I will go with you to a place I know
I will show it to you and delight you

What are you doing young man?
Do you fear there is no place you can go?
I say, young man, there is a place
Of delight to the eye, the ear, to all who delight in the pressed
    linked power of bodies
Go there, young man, and delight in it

I will name that place, I will tell it to your ear
Its name is YMCA
To stay there is fun

My Heart Will Go On

In my dreams, in my sleep, in my deep slumber
I see you, I feel you, I am certain that you continue
I am sustained by your continuation
I am assured of it always

Far, my heart, across spaces
Across distances, across spaces and distances,
Between us, separating us, us two, oceans of distance
O my heart, you continue
I do not doubt that you continue
What is that, my heart, that is opening?
Is it the door, once again, opening?
Yes, it is the door that is opening, once again,
And you are here in my heart and my heart will go on
    indefinitely
Ad infinitum my heart, its heartbeats, and you, continuing.

And the fun continues for the holidays! Leaves of Holly, *Walt's special album of Christmas poems, includes such hits as "Rudolph, My Camerado," "Ho Santa! My Santa!," "Out of the Manger Endlessly Rocking," and "Calamus." If you have not gotten him to leave by the new year, call us, and we will come pick him up.*

How to Pose for Your Civil War Photograph

These are the things that Civil War photographers said to all their customers before the picture was taken, and if you don't believe me, look at the pictures.

L ook sad. No, sadder. No, sadder. No. Look at the camera, but look as though your soul is departing your body as the photograph is being taken. Say, "Everyone I love will soon be dead!" but don't say it with your mouth. Say it with your eyes.

No, look as though the camera has personally wronged you. No, squint more.

Your beard is too groomed. Do you need more facial hair? We have a bunch of it just lying around. It has the texture of ear hair, but it's for your face. You can just sort of affix it wherever you'd like; it doesn't even have to be on a part of your face that makes sense. Do you want an additional eyebrow in a surprising place? Hair that starts out as a sideburn and then becomes something . . . else? We can do that.

Do something weird with your hand. No, weirder. Maybe something Napoleon would do?

Do you want some gloves to hold for no reason?

This group picture is great, folks, but I want half of you to be looking past the camera to the right and the other half of you to be looking past the camera to the left and just one guy in the middle to be making intense, dead-eyed eye contact with the camera.

Brian, if you really feel you need to smile, we should do this shoot out on the battlefield so we can cover up what you're doing with your face with someone's corpse.

Okay, I need some energy from you all! Give me: just got terrible news from home! Give me: the crop has failed! Give me: the cow is dead! Now hold that face and look into the camera!

Jerry, you moved, and now your hand is going to be a blur for the next two hundred years.

The Gettysburg Address, by Aaron Sorkin

I, personally, am glad that Abraham Lincoln wrote the Gettysburg Address—a brief 1863 speech that dedicated a cemetery on that battlefield, reframing the Civil War—and Aaron Sorkin didn't. For everyone else, this piece follows.

Walk with me over this battlefield, Stacy.

Let me tell you a thing or two about this place, right here, where we are standing. Men died here, Stacy. Brave, good men. Men with families.

We're standing on a continent. And you may not know what that means, but I do. It's a landmass, Stacy, on which our forefathers brought forth something. A new nation. Men conceived this nation, Stacy. There was a time when men used to conceive big things—nations! We don't do that anymore.

L. X. X. X. V. I. I. *ellexexexveeayay!* Do you know what that means, Stacy? It's Latin. Means eighty-seven. That's the number of years ago the Founders were. Not so long, when you think of it. Maybe a man's life. Maybe not an important man, maybe not a man you or I would give a second look to, if we passed him on the street, but a man, with a life, and what else is there, in the end?

Now, I don't know much about what the Founders thought, back then. But I can guess. And I'm going to guess. And you're going to listen while I guess, and we should all listen. They had a proposition! A radical proposition. That all men were equal. Not the same. We all know people aren't the same. Some people drive cars, and others ride bicycles. Some men love compromise; other men haven't seen a molehill on which they aren't prepared to die. Some love to make speeches; others are quiet. Taciturn. Reticent. Ungarrulous.

And maybe it's because of those differences that we are now engaged in a great civil war. Maybe those differences are too great for a nation to long endure. Or maybe it's slavery. Maybe not all questions have answers.

But we can agree that we're here now, on that very field. We can agree that we have come here to dedicate, consecrate, hallow, if you will, a portion of this ground. But, Stacy, we can't hallow this ground. These men already did that.

These men did something here that was remarkable.

Maybe people won't remember what we say here. We have ringing words, but they might not ring as loud as the freedom that those men guaranteed for us today. I think they just might, though, because they're by me, Aaron Sorkin.

Anyway, we should be dedicated to their work. We should resolve—no, we should highly resolve—that these dead should not have died in vain, like that man died after eighty-seven years. LXXXVII. Who was that man? Maybe that man was a farmer. Maybe he had a cat, or a bicycle, like you or I, or my wife. Maybe he loved crackers. I think he must have loved something, to stay alive for eighty-seven years. And let me be bold to suggest that that life had a meaning. Just like the lives of the men lying beneath us now, in this hallowed ground.

Eighty-seven years ago, do you know what happened, Stacy? We dreamed big. I don't see us doing that any more. I look around, and I see people who are scared. Scared of seeming nuts. Scared of being fools. Scared that their dialogue will age like an

Andrew Jackson carved from cheese. People who can't handle what we've become. And what have we become, Stacy? Don't we deserve to know? Don't we all deserve that much, at least?

Government of the people, by the people, for the people perishing from the earth isn't cool. You know what would be cool? If it endured. If government of the people, by the people, for the people were to flourish on this earth! You know what would suck? If it perished.

But Other Than That How Was the Play? Audience Feedback for *Our American Cousin*

(PERFORMED AT FORD'S THEATRE,
WASHINGTON, D.C., APRIL 13, 1865)

Five stars. Loved it. Just what I needed to take my mind off the Civil War. Lord Dundreary is so funny!—Peter, Matinee

Five stars. Uproarious! I have never laughed so hard as when Lord Dundreary wondered why sailors were always weighing anchor. "Why the devil won't they keep a memorandum of the weight of their anchor?" Or when the American Cousin said, "Here is a key that will open any lock! A *Yankee*!" before he busts open a locked drawer with an ax. The laughter and applause when Asa (the American Cousin) called one conniving mother a "sockdologizing* old man-trap" was so loud that you could literally have shot a pistol and no one would have heard it. This is what I call real comedy. The Civil War is bad, but at least we are living in a golden age of jokes.—George, Matinee

Five stars. So funny. Lord Dundreary is a laugh riot. When the American Cousin tries to pull the cord to call a servant and turns

---

* This word actually appears in the script.

on the shower instead—I almost urinated myself. This show has everything: physical comedy, wordplay, romance, a drunk butler, a girl who is attractive because she is so good at milking, and an English lord who gets blackmailed because someone finds his bottle of hair dye. I don't know what more you could possibly want. Literally nothing could ruin this play, and I know it'll go down in history for reasons exclusively related to its merit as a work of theater. I can't think of a single situation that wouldn't be made better by seeing this play. If someone is incandescently angry about how this country is going, he should come and watch this play. The guaranteed laughs it provides will make him feel better! —James, Matinee

Five stars. Just what I needed. Thank you Tom Taylor for this masterpiece! I bought up the whole gift shop of Dundreary merchandise afterward! I LOVE *OUR AMERICAN COUSIN*! My only complaint is that I think Florence the female lead and the American Cousin should have gotten together! They had so much chemistry! Maybe in a sequel!?!? COUSINHEADS UNITE! THIS IS THE PLAY WE NEED. —Shelby, Matinee

Five stars. For those of you who are thinking of seeing this play, I say: run, don't walk, to Ford's Theatre! So the plot of the play (spoilers follow) is that Asa Trenchard, a Yankee, is the sole beneficiary of a large English fortune, and he comes to England to claim it, where he meets a bunch of goofy English characters, including Lord Dundreary. Honestly to me the whole play was the Lord Dundreary show; he spends most of it trying to sneeze and failing (VERY FUNNY EVERY TIME AND HAPPENS A LOT OF TIMES), misunderstanding jokes, and trying to get his stolen hair dye back. Cousin Asa uses his

American common sense to poke holes in English pretensions and thwart a money-stealing forced marriage scheme so that true love can prevail, and he sees someone who is milking so successfully that he falls in love with her on the spot. If I wanted to get really picky about it, I would say that he is a confusing pan-American caricature (we do not fall in love with people just because we have seen them milking a single time), but *American Cousin* fans are very toxic, and I don't want to provoke them. Also mostly it's very good! —Sophie, Matinee

Five stars. Fine. Definitely better than the Civil War but not sure why this is the bar we have set for a comedy play. Lord Dundreary was pretty funny, and I liked his Dundrearyisms, but the business where he tried to sneeze and couldn't got old fast. —Louisa, Matinee

Five stars. Very gripping, distracting play that holds an audience's attention and contains many breaks for uproarious laughter so that if hypothetically you wanted to sneak into the theater via a side door and climb into a box, it would be very easy to do that. Actors were only so-so, but not everybody in the world can be a great actor. —John B., Evening

Five stars. I haven't laughed so much in ages. —Walt, Matinee

Five stars. I'm writing this before actually seeing the play, but I can't imagine any reason I'd give it less than five stars! Sounds like the perfect date night. —Mary L.

Big Women

This is an excerpt from Louisa May Alcott's unsuccessful first draft of Little Women, Big Women, *where all the March sisters were sixty feet tall.*

"Christmas won't be Christmas without any presents," grumbled Jo, lying on the enormous rug. Jo was sixty feet tall and people were like ants to her.

"I wish I were a boy," Jo said. "I would go and fight in the war!"

"Do not wish that," Marmee said. "Already the people of this small New England community fear and dread you girls, but if you were male, I genuinely think they would try to kill you."

"But I would be very effective fighting in the Civil War," Jo said. "I could probably turn the tide of the conflict. The cannons are like children's toys to me, and I could pick up the recently designed ironclads and crush them like newspaper boats in my enormous fingers. I could do that even now, if it were not for sexism."

"Be grateful for sexism," Amy said. "I always have been."

Jo sighed.

"Sexism is the only thing keeping us from having to trudge about Antietam in yards and yards of dingy homespun," Amy went on.

"Well, I'll be the man of the family while Father is away, at least," Jo said, boldly lowering her foot, which was the size of an ox-drawn cart, and crushing a man. "Sorry," she said.

The man's friends and relations gathered around his body in horror.

"Jo!" Marmee, her mother, cried.

"You are monsters," the man's friends screamed. "Monsters!"

"Jo is certainly a monster," Amy said, "but I'm not. I'm a lady."

"Ostriches in their large nests agree," sang Beth, the peacemaker, which terrified everyone and caused them to disperse in all directions.

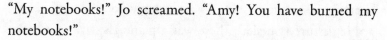

"My notebooks!" Jo screamed. "Amy! You have burned my notebooks!"

It was true. The conflagration was immense. Jo sobbed with rage and frustration.

"But you didn't even write very much in them," Amy said, "because you needed so many sheets of paper to be able to write a single word, even when you wrote it as small as you could."

"That does not make it better!" Jo cried.

"You just wrote the word 'Once,'" Amy said.

"I do not forgive you, and I shall never forgive you," Jo said. "You don't deserve my forgiveness."

Amy nearly drowned by falling through the ice. So did all the inhabitants of the neighboring town, due to the sheer volume of water she displaced.

"I simply must find pickled limes to bring to school," said Amy. "I have incurred a debt to my classmates, and I must repay them in kind!"

Beth smiled. "Follow me," she said, leading Amy to the enormous lime tree behind their house, and the equally enormous vat of brine.

Soon, from the schoolhouse, there came an ominous rumbling and cries of horror. "Amy!" her classmates cried. "The limes are simply too big, and we are all being crushed!" A horse veered left, then right, then halted in the road in a paroxysm of terror, but the rolling lime got it. The carnage was unbelievable.

"Beth," Mr. Laurence said, "I have brought you a piano."

He gestured outside. There was a piano the size of a horse-racing facility. Beth sat down at it and pressed her fingers very gently to its keys and an enormous booming noise echoed through the village and several neighboring villages.

Beth's enormous eyes filled with enormous tears. "I have always wanted to play the piano," she said. "Mr. Laurence, I would embrace you, but—"

"No," Mr. Laurence said, smiling warmly but nervously, "you had better not, I think."

Jo lifted Laurie in her enormous palm so that he was at eye level. "Now," she said, "you must have a good long holiday."

But something in his countenance changed, and she brought him slightly closer to her face to study it better, which prompted a further change in his countenance and sent a shudder through her. "No, Teddy," she said. "Please don't."

"I will, and you must hear me," he answered. "It's no use, we've got to have it out, and the sooner the better for both of us." Jo nearly dropped him but then caught him just in time. "I've loved you ever since I've known you," he went on.

"I wanted to spare you this," Jo said. "I do not love you as you love me."

"Is it because of my size?" Laurie said. "I am fine with our size difference, personally, so if that is what is impeding you, do not let it stand between us."

"It is not that."

"That's really not a problem for me," Laurie said. "It's *really* not."

"Um," Jo said. "You haven't thought this through, Laurie. I would not be a good mistress for your fine house because I am a full twenty feet higher than your fine house. I could not be happy there. I literally cannot fit inside the doors. It is like a tiny dollhouse to me. We would not be happy there because, among other reasons, I would snap the furniture in my enormous fists like kindling."

"I would be happy for you to snap the furniture like kindling," Laurie said.

"There would be nowhere for me to sit down. A woman cannot be happy in her house if there is nowhere for her to sit down. And furthermore I would not fit into society," Jo said, "because the last time I was in society, I stepped on a man with my enormous foot and broke all his ribs."

Laurie made a low sound in the back of his throat that Jo wished very much she had not heard. She politely lowered him to the ground and began to stride back home across the field; her strides were long, and the diminutive figure of Laurie soon dwindled out of sight. *Yikes*, Jo said to herself.

"It is very sad that Beth is dead," John Brooke said.

"Yes," Jo said.

"But she is watching over us from above," said Marmee.

"Even higher above," said Laurie.

"But her piano was a menace to the surrounding communities," John Brooke said. "People heard it for miles, and it frightened them. They did not know the significance of the low haunting sound of three bass notes being struck over and over again in an uncertain manner, and they said, 'Surely it is demons.'"

"She had to practice!" Jo said. "Chopin is not easy, and the sheet music was hard for her to read because it was so small."

Laurie sat contentedly in Amy's pocket. Amy was rowing.

"Amy," Laurie said, tenderly, "we row well together."

"Yes," Amy said. She debated pointing out that she was doing most of the rowing and he was doing none of it, but thought better of it, because marriage was an economic proposition.

"Would you like to be a writer, Jo?" asked Professor Bhaer.

Jo shook her head. "I would like to," she said, "but I do not think it's feasible, given my size."

Excerpt from
Modern Etiquette
(Cursed 1871 edition)

Greetings

You must not greet a strange man on the street. It is improper for a lady to do so, and also, he has no face.

Balls

You must attend several balls each year or you will wither up and die alone, a friendless spinster whom no one remembers, not even your own family.

Card Leaving

In order to socialize, you are required to leave hundreds of cards at people's homes. If you are a mother with a daughter, leave one card. If you are a daughter of a mother, leave two cards. If your father is at the war, leave a card with a black border. If your father wishes to appear to have gone to the war but is hiding in the attic with his second family, leave a black card with a double border. If you are a daughter not born of woman, you must leave three cards, not yours. If you are a woman but not a daughter (such paradoxes occur even in the best-regulated families), you may take a card instead of leaving one. If you are a daughter and do not know what else you are, you may fill a small workbag with cards and use them to create a cardboard doily.

To thank a hostess, leave a card within three days of the event. To leave the hostess in doubt as to whether you enjoyed the festivity, leave a card within two days of the event, but some- one else's card. To indicate to a hostess that you did not enjoy the event, do not leave a card at all, but spit delicately into the card bowl.

Mourning

If anyone has died, you must wear mourning for a year. If you omit mourning and anyone else dies while you have omitted it, their ghost is now your charge. Any ghosts in your charge are not required to leave cards unless they wish to put their names forward for dances.

Pearls are not to be worn in mourning if your loved one was lost at sea; this will make their spirit believe that the sea is taunt- ing them.

Dancing

You must fill your dance card. Any open spaces on your dance card will be filled by ghosts, and it is impolite to refuse a ghost a dance.

You may take refreshment, but not enough refreshment that you have a good time.

The ornamentation of a woman's hair and dress must be simple and becoming, to avoid any repetitions of the Incident. Blondes are to avoid arsenic green; brunettes must dress in rich jewel tones only; redheads must shelter in a root cellar and wait for permission to depart from it to prevent any repetitions of the Incident.

An older woman may wear gayer apparel than a young girl, as she cannot reasonably be mistaken for someone having any fun.

Dining

Men and women must alternate places at table. If the number of places is wrong, it is because the number of men is in excess, and the youngest man should bow to all assembled and announce, "I am going for a walk, and may be some time," before leaving to join a doomed Arctic or Antarctic expedition, whichever is soonest to depart.

You must eat from the smallest fork inward. Nothing can save you if you eat from the largest fork outward, not even God.

That spoon is not for the soup! That spoon is NOT for the soup! That spoon is not for the soup either!

Dessert will occur only if you eat all twenty-three of the courses of capons that precede it.

The finger bowls are for your fingers. Deposit them inside and await further instruction.

Asparagus may be eaten with the bare hands but only when not in mourning. The asparagus, not you.

You must not pass the butter, or you will be turned into a bird and not released until your sister has knit you a sweater from thistledown of the appropriate dimensions.

Mark Twain's Undeath

In addition to writing such novels as The Adventures of Tom Sawyer *and* Huckleberry Finn, *and such travelogues as* Innocents Abroad *and* Roughing It, *Mark Twain was an excruciatingly popular lecturer who loved to unleash a good quip. ("Reports of my death have been greatly exaggerated.") Until the incident. His account follows.*

Reflections Upon Mortality—Attempts at Conversation Returned Unopened—A Bite—Some Dietary Changes Necessary—A Grave Inconvenience—First Sally into New Delicacies—Luxuries of the Post-Cerements Set—On Jaws—A Less Minor Inconvenience—Creditors

Gentlemen, reports of my death have been greatly exaggerated. But reports of my undeath have been exaggerated approximately the correct amount.

The thing came about as follows. I did not set out from the house with the notion in my mind that I was to join the ranks of the living dead. I set out, indeed, with a head thoroughly clear of notions of any kind. I was perambulating in a leisurely manner and taking slow meditative puffs on my cigar when I happened to notice, at a distance, a figure beginning a steady approach. I stood and waited, staring at the horizon. It would have a good effect if I were to say that what I was contemplating was mortality, so—I suppose I shall say that I was doing so! The day of judgment when I shall be held to account for my accounts of what exactly I was contemplating has been indefinitely postponed.

The gentleman whom I had seen approaching now drew level with me. It looked as though he might have eaten something that had not agreed with him. His gait was unsteady, and his eyes bore a glaze. I doffed my hat in greeting in a companionable sort of manner, but he did not take the gesture in the spirit I meant it to be taken. I meant it as a greeting; he perceived it as something in the nature of an invitation, as when the cook rings the dinner bell, as though I had beckoned him to fall to it—upon my unprotected mazzard. He seized me roughly by the shoulder and would have bitten me upon the head had I not shoved him pointedly away.

This was ill done of him, and I told him so in no uncertain terms. I asked him if this was any way to greet a fellow citizen. I asked him if he felt no shame.

But if he felt remorse, he did not show it very largely. He *would* devour the contents of my hat, and if I would not assist him, so much the worse for me. I again endeavored to restrain him, shoving him with, if I may flatter myself, no unmanly measure of force. I had him, at length, at arm's length, when he turned his attention to my arm itself and fell upon it with his teeth. And foul teeth they were, too! I extricated it from him, having made sufficient canine acquaintances over the years to give me practice at this art, and beat a dignified retreat back indoors, where I considered the damage. I was scarcely bleeding, yet conscious of a distinct chill, all along the affected member, which was taking on a paler, more greenish cast.

I rang for my supper.

It was a glorious specimen, when it came! Roast turkey, piping hot, with good green beans, and all the trimmings! Yet I could muster no appetite. It seemed about as appealing as another bite from my rude comrade of the previous hour.

I gazed into my roast turkey. Gentlemen, I must tell you: if you have never gazed into your heaping supper, wondering what in God's name is the *matter* with it—don't begin now. That is my advice to you. The turkey and I contemplated one another, while one of us grew cold and clammy to the touch—and not just one of us, as it would soon appear.

Giving up dinner for a lost cause, I dreaded to ring again for the honest menial who had brought it, quaking inwardly at the prospect of her coming upon it all uneaten. How could she look upon me with anything but horror, a man who would disdain such fine and hearty fare? I dreaded making my explanation to her and determined to postpone it as long as I could. Therefore I set about lighting a cigar. But the d—ed thing wouldn't smoke! The cigar lit, all right. But when I raised it to my lips to puff at it—no puff of smoke appeared!

I began greatly to fear my condition. To turn up my nose at turkey—and now, to fall so short in this matter of the cigar! Very well; I would call for the doctor! I would not suffer this in silence. The cook who had prepared these victuals could not very well hold me to account if I were, as it appeared by these portents, quite at death's door.

Little knowing I was, indeed, at death's door—but on t'other side!

When the doctor did come 'round, he looked very gravely at me. He was one of your spry, small men with bald pates, and I could not suppress the reflection (a very surprising one it was to me, too!) that, all told, that pate of his had a rather *inviting* look to it. I began to feel the stirrings of my appetite returning. That would be the ticket, I reflected, gazing at him. As a medical man, I did not doubt that he would have a robust and juicy brain beneath his cranium—fine sweetmeats indeed! This, too, was an unaccustomed thought. I hoped that it did not show on my countenance.

"What seems to be the trouble?" he inquired, and I informed him about the trouble with the bite, the turkey, and finished with the matter of the cigar. He had begun by taking my pulse—as a formality, no doubt—but I watched him grow more and more puzzled, and finally he swore and averred beneath his breath that this was too many for *him*.

I inquired what was the matter, and he said not to be alarmed, and that he was heartily sorry, but that all indications were that I had no pulse and in all probability had joined the ranks of the undead. I asked him what his fee was, and he offered no very clear answer but began to back toward the door, bowing and doffing his hat and leaving me there alone with my ruminations.

The undead! I had hoped for immortality for my writings, but as for myself, I had no such ambitions, save those of every man who hopes in the Resurrection. And now to find myself in this predicament!

My first weeks in this condition were sorely trying. I found that I did not tire as I had previously, when on walking journeys. I could amble quite comfortably for miles at a time and suffer no ill effects. I have been told that my aroma is peculiar, but I cannot imagine it is any more peculiar than the aromas of some gentlemen I have sat alongside in public conveyances ere now.

Altogether I find fewer things changed than unchanged, save in the matter of cigars and diet. I am experiencing one conundrum, namely: if elements of my memoir were to be published posthumously, what, pray, is to be done with them now? The spirit of posthumous publication would seem to forbid it, but the spirit, I am told, has departed from my mortal coil, and publishers will insist upon their contracts, zombie or no!

I beseeched my creditors, upon having received the intelligence of my altered state, that they would accept my demise as sign that all my debts were paid—but they said they would *not!* They seemed to feel serenely unthreatened by my present state, for all that I growled and menaced, and I don't believe they were far wrong, for what I like to feast on now is *brains*, and Lord knows they are not amply supplied with that victual. So by all accounts I am likely to be upon this circuit until many of my listeners shuffle off their mortal coils, and indeed, longer, until my bones cease to hang together and begin to hang separately—but who knows, then, if I shall not make a more efficient tour of the lecture circuit, with my jawbone in one place and my kneecaps in another. But then, never let it be said that Mark Twain did not make good on his *deaths*.

Branding Session for the Corrupt Bargain of 1877

So, to recap, everyone: we have a deal! Rutherford B. Hayes is going to be the president, even though he lost the popular vote to Samuel Tilden. For a while the Democratic House held up the certification of a winner because enough states had sent confusing, conflicting slates of electors that neither candidate had a clear Electoral College majority. But we finally sat down at Wormley's Hotel and made a bargain! In exchange for becoming president, Hayes has agreed to pull all remaining federal troops out of the Southern states, ending Reconstruction and ushering in a nightmarish time for the Black populations of the former Confederacy. He is also going to make a Southern Democrat the postmaster general, and maybe he will even fund a railroad that the South thinks will help boost its economy? Who knows! So we have a lot to work with here. What name are we thinking this will wind up with in the history books?

The Corrupt Bargain? Okay, certainly a start. Any other names? I think that's already the election of 1824.

The Corrupt Bargain of 1877? Yeah, basically the same idea, but I guess it's got the date there now.

Huh. Surely there must be something else. I understand that this is a very accurate description of what is going on here, but our job is not to accurately describe history; it is to confuse people about the events leading up to and following the Civil War, incepting a fantasy of Southern chivalry, so that later they will produce the novel and film *Gone with the Wind* and generally be surprised anytime there is still racism.

I understand that this is ending Reconstruction! Still, just from a branding perspective, it seems like calling it "the corrupt bargain" is really not optimal! "The Compromise of 1850" sounds neutral and *that* included the Fugitive Slave Act and effectively spread slavery to the entire country! I personally think we should rebrand 1850 as "the corrupt bargain" and call our thing "the Compromise of 1877."

Okay. Fine. What about "the bargain that just happened"? That feels neutral. "The Wormley's Hotel Bargain?" Of 1877?

Just—if we go through and look at all the branding that has happened, I think this is an unforced error. We have *absolutely* been winning the branding war up to this point. I may be wrong about this, but I thought we had set it up so that when history textbooks talked about white people who supported Reconstruction, they would refer to Northerners as "carpetbaggers" and Southerners as "scalawags"? You know these are insults, right? Yet these are the terms that keep showing up! It would be as though I called all the people who disagreed with me politically "Dickheads" and history texts just . . . went along with it! and were like "1870 marked the arrival of the Dickheads in national politics." This is the power we wield!

And we're going to call the agreement that helped put an end to everything the "Scalawags" and "Carpetbaggers" were struggling for . . . the Corrupt Bargain? We even call the people trying to end Reconstruction the Redeemers, which sounds WAY nicer than People Fighting to End Black Citizenship Rights Through the Use of Intimidation and Violence. "Redeemers" sounds either vaguely religious or like they're really into coupons.

To be frank, if we can turn the LITERAL Confederacy, whose entire raison d'être was to keep slavery, into "The Lost Cause," we should not be settling for "The Corrupt Bargain" here. Don't get me started on States' Rights! And we're going to throw all these triumphs of elision away for . . . the Corrupt Bargain of 1877?

Sure, not all our brands have been successful. We didn't get anywhere with the Know-Nothing Party, but they were giving us nothing, and it's still better than "A Strange Amalgam of Religious Bigots and Xenophobes" (our other best option).

Just seems like across the board we're winning this branding war, and here we are throwing in the towel without a fight. But if nobody has anything better, I guess we can pencil in Corrupt Bargain.

Okay see you in twenty years to put up a big beautiful statue of a Lost Cause figure!

One other tiny note: the Electoral Count Act seems very confusing! I'm sure this won't come up again, but are we absolutely sure it's written in such a way that if somebody wanted to act in bad faith and overturn the results of the election, they couldn't find any justification for that? It seems like kind of a mess. Just thought I'd mention it! Anyway, someone else's problem! Have a great Thursday, everyone.

Nikola Tesla's Friends Intervene (A PowerPoint)

I have been feeding pigeons, thousands of them, for years. . . . But there was one pigeon, a beautiful bird, pure white with gray tips on its wings; that one was different. It was female. I would know that pigeon anywhere. I had only to wish and call her and she would come flying to me. She understood me, and I understood her. I loved that pigeon. Yes, I love that pigeon, as a man loves a woman, and she loved me. . . . As long as I had her, there was purpose to my life. . . . When that pigeon died, something went out of my life. . . . I knew that my life's work was finished.

—*Actual Nikola Tesla Quote*

I Think Tesla Is Dating a Pigeon

and We Need to Stage an Intervention

WHAT

- Our friend Nikola Tesla is dating a pigeon.

WHO

- We all know Nikola Tesla, the genius inventor and pioneer of alternating current.
- Used to work for Edison?
- Invented all the things that Marconi invented
- Has a little mustache
- Makes it work

The Pigeon Situation

- Nikola has always been very vocally opposed to marriage, saying that no married man ever accomplished anything (?).
- So when he said he had "found someone" and "was happy," I was all set to be excited for him, provided that what he had found was in fact a person and not, say, a pigeon.
- But I think it's a pigeon.

Evidence That Suggests It's a Lady

- Nikola calls her "she."
- Says he "knows she loves him," which I don't even think we know if pigeons are capable of love so that's a big argument for it not being a pigeon.

Evidence That Suggests It's a Pigeon

- All Nikola's friends are pigeons.
- Have we ever seen anyone who wasn't a pigeon visiting Nikola?
- Remember that time Nikola asked the hotelkeeper to prepare a fancy breakfast for his friends and the breakfast was birdseed because his friends were all pigeons?
- Nikola says he loves her "as a man loves a woman" which you wouldn't have to specify if it were just a woman.
- I asked if she was a pigeon, and Nikola said "I bet you don't believe that love between a man and a pigeon is possible the same way that a man and woman love each other," which, again, you would not say if it weren't a pigeon.
- I pointed out that he hadn't actually stated that she wasn't a pigeon, and Nikola said, "I will tell you that such love is possible! Love between a man and pigeon is a beautiful kind of love, the kind that even Darwin himself embraced, and Darwin was a man of science, as I am!"
- Nikola went on a long tirade about how Shakespeare's Dark Lady sonnets were actually addressed to a pigeon with distinctive plumage and he was going to prove it, which would have been completely unrelated if his new woman is a woman but would make sense if she were, in fact, a pigeon.

Evidence That Suggests It's a Pigeon, Continued

- I asked what parts about her he liked, and he said "beak" without hesitation.
- But then he saw how startled I was and corrected it to "plumage."
- Finally he said "voice," but at that point things felt like they were very strongly in the pigeon camp.
- Women don't have beaks or plumage.
- I asked when he had last seen her, and he said "when she flew into my window," which, again, a woman would not be able to do.
- I asked how they met, and he said "I put out some birdseed and that attracted her," which, to be fair, could have happened with a woman but I feel like the Occam's Razor explanation here is that it was a pigeon.
- Timothy said, "I just want you to know, Nikola, that if she is a pigeon, I will still support you," and then Nikola said, "Thank you, Timothy, that means a lot!" which he would have no reason to say if she weren't a pigeon.

Evidence That Could Go Either Way

- Nikola says she has a beautiful voice.
- Nikola says she hates cats.
- Nikola describes her as "most active during the daytime."
- Nikola says she's a "biped possessing a soul."

Should We Do Something About It? Why Not Just Let the Man Live?

- Think how much of a win this would be for Thomas if he learned that Nikola Tesla is in love with a bird.
- We CANNOT let Edison win.
- Nikola can do better than this bird.
- We don't know the motives of the bird—she could be trying to charm him into bequeathing her his valuable patents.

Other Edison Ideas

Genius is 1 percent inspiration and
99 percent perspiration.

—*Thomas Alva Edison*

Inventions to work on:

1. Something you rub on yourself to make yourself sweat less

2. Something you rub on yourself to make yourself sweat more (more ideas)

3. Cool slogan about how sweating more is good for having ideas

4. Cooling device for the indoors

5. Bucket that dumps water on the person you're talking to so they also look wet and it is less noticeable how sweaty you are

6. Warm woolen thing you can put on the body to encourage more sweating

7. Drenched towelette

8. Moist towelette

9. Contest for who can have the wettest T-shirt that can become a known cultural phenomenon so that people will assume you could have multiple reasons for having a shirt that is wet

10. Moisture-wicking T-shirt for a sweaty guy

11. Way of getting breeze into a room

12. Device to make you less frightened of things so that you can eliminate nervous sweat and just have regular temperature sweat

13. Winter

14. Fan of some kind for the man who is covered in sweat

15. Big block of ice

16. Absorbent towel you can put in your bed so your sheets don't get ruined when you sweat a lot

17. Really sweaty light bulb

18. Light bulb

Nellie Bly Reviews Blackwell's Island

Nellie Bly was a pioneering journalist who went undercover at Blackwell's Island, an institution for the mentally ill, in 1887 and revealed all manner of abuses.

Nellie Bly:

If it were possible to give this a lower review than 0 out of five stars, that is what I would give it.

Let me begin by saying that I thought it was going to be very difficult to fool people into believing that I was mentally ill. I thought, I will have to make some strange faces, and I will have to really act in order for these doctors (who are undoubtedly experts) to conclude that someone as obviously *compos mentis* as I am needs to be locked away.

But actually it turns out that it is very easy! All I did was not have money and be female and occasionally speak Spanish, and everyone quickly concluded that I was probably insane. Actually, I was much more worried about getting out successfully than I was about getting in successfully. This seems like a pretty fundamental problem for an insane asylum to have, and I think they ought to fix it.

One of the inmates I got to know was clearly completely sane but could speak only German, and nobody would translate for her or let her out. Another had just been treated for nervous debility and was supposed to be somewhere she could recover;

needless to say, this was a bad place for that. Still another woman that I talked to was just French and had nothing else wrong with her that I could detect.

Everyone was forced to take freezing-cold baths and was subjected to brutal scrubbing in a communal tub full of dirty water, using the same towel for people with sores and people without. We were sent to bed cold and wet with inadequate bedding. The food was horrible: hard bread covered in inedible butter, occasional spoiled meat or fish served without any salt whatsoever, and undrinkable tea. We were made to sit on a bench for hours at a time with no entertainment or stimulation of any kind. Then we were taken out for walks during which no one was allowed to pick up anything, and some women were chained together with belts. At night, nurses came and made lots of noise checking on the inmates so that it was impossible for us to sleep even if we had wanted to. This sort of treatment is enough to leave even a mentally well-adjusted woman at the end of her rope and I believe it ought to be stopped at once. I do not recommend Blackwell's Island.

Blackwell's Island responds:

Nellie! We are so sorry to hear about your negative experience.

To respond point by point: We are very sorry about the language mishap! The number-one sign of being insane is speaking in tongues (French, German, Spanish). German is the most worrisome of all the languages; we have a nurse here at this institution who is German and ought to be able to speak German to the patients to translate for them, but she refuses to, and that is quite right of her. Wanting to speak a language other than English is a terrifying sign of mental derangement.

Another sign of being insane is if you do not have any money.

A third sign of being insane is if you demand to be tested by a doctor to determine if you are insane. Why would a sane person think to ask about this?

You complained about the freezing-cold baths, bad food, lack of exercise, lack of engaging activities, and sleep deprivation.

To this I say: pick a lane, Nellie! First you complain that none of the people you encountered in the asylum seemed insane enough, and then you complain about the steps we are taking to fix that. Which is it?

Look, our job is to run an insane asylum. How can we do that if all the people in it are not insane, just German? That's why we developed our innovative combination of freezing baths, sleep deprivation, boredom, and bad food: to make sure that everyone we house is in the worst mental state possible! That's a Blackwell's Island promise. However, we do hear what you're saying: an inspector might frown on these practices. Now, whenever an inspector visits, we are going to give everyone clean clothes right before they arrive, and we are buying a big barrel of salt to display prominently in the kitchen.

Also, every specific individual whose plight you mentioned in your article has mysteriously vanished in the night, got better, or we never heard of them and think you made them up. Please choose the excuse best suited to each case.

We would like to offer you a free stay at Blackwell's Island anytime you would like to experience our improved customer services.

50 States of Grey

Grover Cleveland surrounded him. Grover Cleveland was in front of him, and Grover Cleveland was behind him. He was entirely hemmed in by the mustached Ohioan bulk of Grover Cleveland. He was the twenty-third president, Benjamin Harrison, and on either side of him, Grover Cleveland was serving noncontiguous terms.

The Yellow Wallpaper Guy Tries to Get a Refund

Viewed one way, The Yellow Wallpaper *by Charlotte Perkins Gilman is a story about a woman who is tormented and not taken seriously by her husband or her doctor. Viewed another way, it is about a guy who has the worst possible wallpaper-purchasing experience.*

Hello, Home Goods!

Hey hello, yes I have a complaint.

And what's the product you're calling about today?

Wallpaper. Yellow wallpaper.

Hold on a second let me transfer you to wall coverings.

Hello, I am calling about some yellow wallpaper I purchased from your store. The wallpaper injured me, and I believe I am entitled to compensation.

The wallpaper injured you?

A man should be able to leave his wife utterly alone in a room for a few days and not worry that the wallpaper is going to irreparably break her mind.

I'm sorry to hear that your experience with the wallpaper wasn't positive.

That is an understatement. Hear that? The low, smooching thumping noise? That's my wife. Just going around and around the wall. There is a woman in the wallpaper she says.

She wants to let the woman out of the wallpaper or possibly get into the wallpaper herself, and in the process of doing this she ran me over several times when I had fallen to the floor in a dead faint.

I'm sorry to hear that. We want all our wallpaper customers to have a spectacular experience.

We didn't mean to buy the wallpaper with a woman in it. We just wanted regular wallpaper. Does all the yellow wallpaper come with a woman in it? Maybe I can buy a different kind of wallpaper?

Would you like a different brand of yellow wallpaper?

Or just paint if that's easier, we aren't married to wallpaper. Indeed, I may not be married to anyone.

I'm sorry to hear that, sir. Hang on I'll transfer you to the paint department.

L. Frank Baum's
Dystopian YA Novel

A popular thesis holds that The Wizard of Oz *by L. Frank Baum was an allegorical critique of American monetary policy. The yellow brick road was the gold standard, the cowardly lion was William Jennings Bryan, and Dorothy's silver slippers were—bimetallism, somehow. Is this definitely what L. Frank Baum meant? Well, here is a draft of L. Frank Baum's rejected young adult novel, also about the gold standard, that I think makes things a lot clearer.*

Dot couldn't believe it was already almost the Culling, the time when all the residents of the Farm States gathered to be sorted into their personality groups for life. She sighed and rubbed some farm dirt across her wind-chafed face, which was beautiful but not so much that she was unapproachable. It was on days like the Culling when she wished that both her parents had not died under mysterious circumstances. She wished she could have had their advice, or known what Personality Groups they belonged to. She was being raised by her aunt and uncle. They were both Greenbacks, the Personality Group that meant that they were hardworking but no one knew how to value them. Secretly, Dot hoped that she would not be assigned to this Personality Group, even though she knew that was vain and shallow of her.

"Hey, Dot," said Bry, interrupting her reverie. Bry lived next door. There was just something about him that was different. "Are you excited for the Culling?"

Dot pushed her hair out of her face. "It's the only thing I think about," she said. "It's the only event we have here."

"A fixed, standard event." Bry rolled his eyes. They were green with flecks of gold in them, like some people had unsuccessfully argued that currency should be. "Bo-ring. Nothing so boring as a fixed standard."

Dot glanced around nervously. "Fixed standards are what keep our society together," she hissed through her teeth. She pushed some more hair out of her face. "That's why we have to have the Culling. That's why we have Greenbacks, and, and the Gold Standard, and work so hard to protect the Reserve, and the Mint. That's the Way, Bry, you know that."

"Ever stop to wonder *why* it's the Way?" Bry asked. He pushed some hair out of his face this time, then slouched, deliberately, in a way that would be bad for his back later but looked cool now.

"Bry," Dot said, glancing nervously around, "you know we can't question the Way."

"I question it," Bry said. His shirt unbuttoned itself just a little bit. "I question everything. Maybe what we need is for things to be free. Maybe there's more to life than just being told your Personality Group is Gold Standard." He lowered his voice to a whisper. It was soft, like a forbidden monetary policy. "Maybe there's another, secret group you've never even heard of. Free Coinage of Silver."

Dot gasped and covered his mouth with a hand. "You can't say things like that, Bry!" she said.

A man cleared his throat behind them. It was her uncle. He leaned heavily on a pitchfork. "I guess now is as good a time as any to tell you how your parents died," he said. He squinted off into the middle distance. "I'm sure you must have guessed by now. Noticing little things about yourself. How you don't quite fit in with us simple Greenbacks. Well, they were both Free Silverites."

"I'd never even heard of Free Silver until this morning," Dot said, "and now I've heard of it twice!"

"They were both Free Silverites," her uncle continued, leaning even more heavily on his pitchfork, "until the day they died. I suppose now is as good a time as any to tell you how."

"Yes," Dot said, uncertainly, "although, of course, you shouldn't, if you don't feel like it."

"Well," her uncle said, "I reckon I will." He leaned even harder on the pitchfork so that the whole fork portion of it was now deeply embedded in the ground. "They were crushed," he said, blinking back tears, "by an oversize gold coin. Pushed by President McKinley himself."

Dot sobbed. Bry held her. "I swear," Dot said, "when the Culling comes, I'm going to get my revenge. On the whole system. I'll burn it to the ground if I have to."

"That's good," Bry said. "You've taken your first step into a larger world."

Dot nodded bravely and pushed more hair out of her face. This time it wasn't even her hair. She was mildly alarmed by it.

"I'm also a werewolf," Bry added, "but there was never a good time to mention it so I didn't." His shirt opened completely. "Until now."

The Group Telegram Following the "Cross of Gold" Speech

Monetary policy! Everybody at the end of the nineteenth century cared about it, even people who weren't L. Frank Baum.

As usual, the question boiled down to: do you want things to be easier for people who OWE money, or for people who ARE OWED money? The Democrats favored free silver. This would mean you could take silver to a mint and turn it into coins—the way you could with gold. At the time, raw silver was valuable but not as valuable as the silver coins would be. If they permitted you to coin silver, you could make yourself much richer with a visit to the mint. Understandably, people with debts and lots of silver (silver mine owners, many farmers in the West) thought the free coinage of silver was a terrific idea. People who were owed money, like business types in the Northeast, thought this sounded suspicious.

This was a big issue. And someone who deeply cared about it was William Jennings Bryan, who famously delivered a speech to the Democratic National Convention in 1896 about it. The speech, remembered for its line about mankind being crucified on a "Cross of Gold," was rapturously received. Except by this one group telegram.

OKAY, I'M JUST GOING TO SAY IT STOP
DID ANYBODY ELSE THINK THAT WAS A LITTLE
WEIRD? STOP
I'LL SHUT UP IF NOBODY DID STOP
BUT I'M NOT CRAZY, RIGHT? STOP

I THOUGHT IT WAS A MOVING SPEECH STOP

MOVING IS AN UNDERSTATEMENT!!!!!! STOP

WOW YOU DICTATED EACH OF THOSE EXCLAMATION
POINTS INDIVIDUALLY STOP

YES BECAUSE I FELT SO EMPHATICALLY ABOUT IT
STOP
WAIT AM I ALONE HERE? STOP

IT WAS A VERY MOVING SPEECH ABOUT HOW BAD
THE GOLD STANDARD WOULD BE STOP

YES LEONARD I KNOW THAT'S THE LITERAL
CONTENT OF THE SPEECH STOP
WE NEED BIMETALLISM. IF THE REPUBLICAN
PLATFORM SAYS THAT THEY WOULD BE WILLING
TO ADOPT BIMETALLISM IF EUROPE ADOPTS IT,
THEN EVEN THEY ADMIT WE NEED BIMETALLISM
STOP THE WORKING MAN WILL BENEFIT FROM
BIMETALLISM STOP THE NOTION THAT THE
PROSPERITY BROUGHT TO THE OWNERS OF
BUSINESS BY THE GOLD STANDARD WILL SOMEHOW
TRICKLE DOWN TO THE WORKING MAN IS BOGUS,

GIVING MORE MONEY TO THE WORKING MAN WILL
FLOW OUT IMMEDIATELY INTO THE ECONOMY AND
BENEFIT EVERYONE AND WE AS DEMOCRATS HAVE
ALWAYS BELIEVED THIS AND THROWN OUR LOT IN
WITH THE LABORER STOP
I GOT ALL OF THAT STOP
I AM TALKING ABOUT THE OTHER CAN YOU DO
ITALICS WITH A TELEGRAM NO I DON'T WANT THIS
TO BE PART OF THE TELEGRAM I JUST WANTED TO
KNOW IF OTHER COULD BE IN ITALICS OKAY WELL
I GUESS SEND IT AND I'LL START THE SENTENCE
OVER STOP
I AM TALKING ABOUT THE OTHER PART STOP

I LAUGH ALOUD AT YOUR PREVIOUS TELEGRAM STOP

I'M TALKING ABOUT THE PART WHERE WILLIAM
JENNINGS BRYAN CLEARLY WANTED TO HAVE SEX
WITH THE GOLD STANDARD STOP
LIKE YOU DIDN'T FIND IT AT ALL WEIRD THAT WE
SORT OF GRADUALLY SEGUED FROM HIS STIRRING
APPEAL TO THE COMMON MAN ABOUT MONETARY
POLICY TO THIS LIKE, WEIRD CRUCIFIXION FANTASY
INVOLVING THE GOLD STANDARD STOP
I DID NOT CONSENT TO BE PART OF THAT AND I FELT
LIKE HE AND THE GOLD STANDARD SHOULDN'T
HAVE INVOLVED US IN IT STOP

DOT DOT DOT STOP

YOU DIDN'T THINK IT WAS AT ALL WEIRD THAT HE

STOOD THERE FOR FIVE SECONDS WITH HIS ARMS
STRETCHED OUT STOP
TO INDICATE TO US HOW IT WOULD LOOK IF THE
GOLD STANDARD HAD ITS WAY WITH HIM STOP

HMM OKAY NO I'M THINKING ABOUT IT MORE AND
I'M STARTING TO SHARE YOUR CONCERN STOP

WE'RE ALL SITTING THERE IN TOTAL SILENCE STOP
AND WILLIAM JENNINGS THE FUCK BRYAN IS
STANDING THERE INFLICTING HIS GOLD STANDARD
FANTASIES ON THE WHOLE CHICAGO COLISEUM
FULL OF DELEGATES TO THE DEMOCRATIC NATIONAL
CONVENTION STOP
"YOU SHALL NOT PRESS DOWN UPON THE BROW OF
LABOR THIS CROWN OF THORNS" STOP
OKAY WILLIAM! STOP
"YOU SHALL NOT CRUCIFY MANKIND UPON A CROSS
OF GOLD" STOP
I'M LOOKING OVER AT FORMER MASSACHUSETTS
GOVERNOR WILLIAM E. RUSSELL AND HE'S LOOKING
BACK LIKE WHAT IS THIS STOP
PITCHFORK BEN TILLMAN DID A LITTLE, THAT
THING WHERE YOU MAKE THE NOISE OF A WHIP,
AND HE WASN'T WRONG TO DO SO STOP

LEONARD IS TYPING STOP

LOOK I WAS FULLY ON BOARD WITH ALL THE STUFF
ABOUT THE COMMON LABORER NEEDING A LOOSER
MONETARY POLICY STOP

LEONARD HAS ENTERED TEXT STOP

ALTHOUGH IF ANYTHING WILLIAM JENNINGS BRYAN
SEEMS LIKE HE WANTS A TIGHTER MONETARY
POLICY STOP

NO GOLD STANDARD DON'T . . . STOP STOP

IMAGINE A VISAGE BUT WINKING STOP

LEONARD STOP STOP

IF YOU WERE A HARD MONETARY STANDARD WOULD
YOU HOLD YOURSELF AGAINST ME STOP

I GUESS I JUST WANTED TO ASK IF IT WAS WEIRD
FOR ANYONE ELSE STOP

DEFINITELY WEIRD I WON'T LOOK AT FREE SILVER
THE SAME WAY EVER AGAIN STOP

WAIT ARE WE FOR OR AGAINST THE GOLD
STANDARD NOW STOP

NO BIMETALLISM IS STILL GOOD POLICY I JUST FEEL
WEIRD ABOUT IT NOW STOP

We're the Rhinoceroses Trying to Keep Teddy Roosevelt's Life Together

Teddy "Speak Softly and Carry a Man, a Plan, a Canal, Panama!" Roosevelt was the youngest man to serve as president. He was enormously energetic and did A Lot, perhaps The Most, not all of it good. Whenever he got stressed (and sometimes just for fun), he would go off and kill huge volumes of large game mammals. Here are the notes that some of them left behind.

A ugust 1913: We have failed in our mission. I leave these notes for those who will come after us. May they profit by our example.

1897

I have arrived at Teddy Roosevelt's house. I am a rhinoceros in disguise. The council sent me. One thing is clear to us: Now is not the time to be timid and criticize what the rhinoceros in the arena is doing. Now is the time to involve ourselves in the crises of our era. That is why we have chosen this path, a path of action.

We rhinos have noticed a distressing pattern. Whenever Theodore Roosevelt encounters a setback, his sole means of emotional expression is to embark on a rugged trek and shoot as many large game mammals as he possibly can. We have all lost loved ones to his periods of distress—first, after the loss of his father; next when both his wife and his mother died within hours of each other. As large game mammals, it is therefore in our interest to prevent anything else from going wrong in Teddy Roosevelt's life.

I have accepted this dangerous assignment and taken cover in the Roosevelt residence posing as a coatrack. My colleague Rhadamanthus is pretending to be a hassock. So far all is well. The only difficulty is all the rhino heads already in the house. Over the staircase I see the dead, unseeing eyes of my friend Marius, his face frozen in a rictus grin. He was so young. He had so much hope. Teddy took that from him. A gruesome sight, but it steels me to my task. We simply cannot fail.

1898

Teddy is advancing in politics splendidly! The men in smoke-filled rooms are quite struck by him. Members of the New York Republican machine have been sitting on me all night, mistaking me for an ottoman. One of them put out his cigar on me. It is fortunate that I have a thick hide. Rhadamanthus snorted, but there was enough snorting in the room already that nobody took any notice. Indeed, it went so well that we had hoped to see Teddy ascend to the presidency. But then they went with someone else instead.

I suggested filling the room with even more smoke, but that didn't help. Now poor Rhadamanthus has developed a horrible cough.

1900

Minor disruption. Teddy has done too much work against machine politics and the bosses have determined to send him somewhere he can do no more harm. They have settled on the post of the vice presidency.

Teddy seems in good spirits, speaks of perhaps attending law school while in Washington, as his job will offer little to hold his interest. But his gaze strays often to the guns on the wall.

Spoke to Rhadamanthus; he too fears the worst. This man wants to be the bride at every wedding and the corpse at every funeral. He will not do well in the vice presidency. We must devise some distraction for Teddy, something to occupy his mind.

1901

Rhadamanthus and I have arrived at a somewhat unorthodox solution to our problem involving a firearm and an anarchist. President McKinley, we hope, will understand.

1902

Minor disruption: his daughter, Alice, has taken up smoking. "Not under my roof!" Teddy thundered. We do not like anything to distress him. While Alice was napping on Rhadamanthus, I hoisted them both onto my back, and with enormous effort and use of a winch we were able to transport her on top of the roof. As long as she smokes above it rather than beneath it, Theodore cannot possibly find fault. Rhadamanthus says I am too literal, but I am determined to make what gains we can.

1904

Wonderful news! Teddy has been reelected president on his own steam. This should keep him pleasantly occupied for many years.

We are helping to stampede some bills through Congress to preserve national parks. All is well.

1905

How quickly joy withers on the vine. Teddy has vowed not to run for reelection. Stricken by the announcement, Rhadamanthus left his hassock post and began rumbling down the Mall toward the Washington Monument, saying that he would ram it until it fell. But it did not budge, and his horn is bent. I stood with him while he grunted in impotent rage. He feels, as I do, that this will bring calamity for us all, and sooner than we'd like. Our only hope is for Roosevelt to run again. But when can that be? Perhaps he can take the words back. Perhaps we can find other sources of fulfillment to enrich his life. But even as I write this, a shudder runs through me. Marius's empty eyes meet mine with accusation. For this man, it is politics or nothing.

1906

He set aside a national park. It was nice. We asked the resident bears there for help or advice; they merely growled. Time is running out.

1909

It is as we feared. Departing the presidency has left him unmoored, and seeing Taft take the oath of office broke him. Sleet fell during the speeches. Pathetic fallacy, perhaps?

Grim times await. Teddy has departed on a hunting expedition for the Smithsonian. There is nothing for Rhadamanthus and myself to do but to await the butcher's bill. We do not doubt it will be high.

1910

Eleven thousand specimens. That is the toll of dead. He has brought the corpses to the Smithsonian to be displayed for the edification of the public. Rhadamanthus has lost his dear mother, and I have lost my two nieces. Our private griefs can only hint at the general devastation. We should despair, but our resolution is firmer than ever. We have failed once. We cannot fail a second time. Teddy Roosevelt must never suffer again.

1912

Teddy Roosevelt is running for president against Taft. It is delusional, perhaps, but not impossible. We are working beyond all measure of exhaustion. The Moose Coalition out west has sent several representatives and have consented to pose for his campaign literature, but I have grave misgivings. Rhadamanthus and I think frequently of the slaughter of 1910. Sometimes I find myself glassy-eyed even when I'm *not* pretending to be a coat rack. Rhadamanthus fares even worse. He looks pale and drawn.

His hide has loosened, making him difficult to sit on. No one likes a saggy hassock. I fear for us both.

I consider if I can summon the courage to do to Teddy what we did to McKinley. Why should we guard his life when he is so careless with ours? I shall not tell Rhadamanthus. I must bear the moral burden alone.

1912

My plan has failed. The gunman hit Roosevelt, but the bullet stuck in his speech. If he delivered shorter speeches, we might be able to breathe more easily. He continues unabated on the stump. But the campaign is flagging. Rhadamanthus suspects what I have done. I expected him to reproach me, but he merely sighed. "I would have done the same, Artaxerxes," he told me, "if I had the strength." He speaks with a wheeze; too much smoke, too many rooms. There is little fight left in either of us. My only consolation is the hope that nobody could possibly wish to vote for Woodrow Wilson. May Roosevelt prevail!

1912

He has not prevailed. Wilson takes the day. Teddy now makes plans for an expedition to the River of Doubt. Our failure could not possibly be greater.

Teddy Roosevelt will never be appeased. Teddy Roosevelt is too active to be stopped. If my family must perish at his hands, then I shall perish with them. I am going home.

Why the National Parks Were Set Aside

"Leave it as it is. You cannot improve on it. The ages have been at work on it, and man can only mar it." This is what Teddy Roosevelt said about the Grand Canyon. A likely story. But what about the other national parks? Why were they set aside?

Yellowstone: GEYSTER SQUIRTS HUGE AMOUNTS OF WATER INTO AIR WITHOUT WARNING; PEOPLE MUST BE KEPT AWAY.

Sequoia: HUGE TREES! Extremely dangerous.

Yosemite: This place is full of glacial rocks, and they could fall on people at any time! Some of them are steep, and people might try to climb them and get hurt. There are also waterfalls, which combine heights (danger) and water (still a dangerous substance even if it comes free with the planet).

Mount Rainier: Name sounds dangerously wet.

Crater Lake: Deceptively appealing, crystal clear water! Huge drowning hazard.

Wind Cave: I'm just scared of caves generally, and this is a very big cave.

Mesa Verde: This seems very historical, and people might break things.

Glacier Park: Too beautiful; people might be overcome. Also big body of clear water; as established, water is dangerous.

Rocky Mountain: I think I saw a moose there.

Hawaii Volcanoes: Has volcanoes in it. Uh, VOLCANOES?!?

Haleakala: Has what it says is dormant volcanoes, but how are they sure?

Bryce Canyon: Who is this Bryce, and why does he get a whole canyon to himself? Sounds like people ought to keep away.

Badlands: Says bad right in the name, in both English and French, and in the original name given to it by the Lakota people.

Petrified Forest: Why are these trees so scared? What did they see?!? We must prevent anyone else from seeing it.

Big Thicket: Sounds very easy to get lost in, don't want anyone taking that risk.

Zion: Seems steep.

Waco Mammoth: There is a mammoth in the name; enough said.

Carlsbad Caverns: Carl says they are bad, and I trust Carl.

Great Smoky Mountain: This mountain is on fire!

Hot Springs: CAUTION! HOT.

Everglades: THIS IS IN FLORIDA.

Saguaro: Very sharp violent plant.

Theodore Roosevelt: We know for certain that this site produced Theodore Roosevelt once; we cannot take that risk again.

Redwood: More big trees trying to sneak by under another name.

Dry Tortugas: Something has gone wrong with these tortugas.

Gateway Arch: Clearly this arch leads to other more dangerous arches.

Joshua Tree: See U2 album.

Great Sand Dunes: I hate sand; it's coarse, rough, irritating, and it gets everywhere.

Indiana Dunes: Sad for these lesser dunes.

New River Gorge: This was set aside in 2020; there should not be any new rivers.

Death Valley: HARD NO.

Grand Canyon: Big hole in the ground without proper signage. Leave it as it is.

The Jungle, Basically

Upton Sinclair's The Jungle *is a novel about conditions in the meatpacking industry. I hear you asking: novels have all kinds of characters and themes. How could people tell this 1906 novel was about conditions in the meatpacking industry? Was it subtle? Well, no. No, it wasn't. Here is how it went.*

The young man Jurgis Rudkus arrived in the city of Chicago. Once he had been a baby in Lithuania. He had been a normal-looking baby, good and strong, with little plump fingers that looked like sausages, which was foreshadowing. But now he was an adult, in the city of Chicago, where the meatpacking industry was.

It was not actually a jungle. But metaphorically it was a jungle. It was a jungle in the sense that if someone said, "Is this a good place to get a sandwich from?" you would say, "No. Do not get a sandwich there."

Jurgis left the tenement where he lived with other named characters. He was about to run into the woman he would love for the rest of his days. It would be a meet cute, the only time any meat in Chicago had ever been cute, because the conditions in the meatpacking industry there were so bad.

Jurgis strolled down the Chicago street when he stumbled and walked right into a beautiful woman. She was holding a big bundle of meat, and when she collided with Jurgis, she dropped all the meat onto the dirty Chicago sidewalk.

"You dropped this," he said.

Their eyes locked unexpectedly, without warning, as the dangerous machinery that Jurgis worked with all day in the meatpacking industry sometimes did. Jurgis worried about that machinery.

"Oh," she said, "that's fine. I'm Ona. I work in the meatpacking industry in Chicago."

Jurgis looked at her and felt a trembling, warm sensation all over his body. He hoped that it was love and not the aftereffects of the "Chicago meat sandwich" he had recently eaten, which, when he thought about it further, was not at all a sufficiently detailed label for a sandwich.

"Is that a sausage in your pocket," Ona asked, "or are you just happy to see me?"

"It is a sausage," Jurgis said. "I work in the meatpacking industry in Chicago."

"We are married now," Ona said to Jurgis. "A link that can never be severed."

"Do not say a link," Jurgis said. "I have seen sausage being made here in Chicago, where we live and pack meat, and I know all too well how easily a link may be severed."

In the bedroom, they looked at each other. He touched her all over with his bare hands, discovering her most tender places, like he would do to an ox carcass at the meatpacking plant where he worked. The conditions in the meatpacking plant were bad.

They lay with their loins all tangled together on the floor in a room that smelled vaguely of mouse droppings. No one paid them any money afterward, though they had been at it for a considerable time and exerted themselves greatly. "Wow," Ona said. "This is really exactly like work."

"I am pregnant," Ona said. She thrilled at the feeling of something small and alive stirring inside her, just the way someone who had eaten recently produced Chicago meat would not.

Ona screamed. She was giving birth. It was a baby.

The doctor wrapped him up very well and handed him to her.

"Take the baby home and age him," the doctor added. "Do not put him in an airtight container." Ona nodded solemnly, but a chill of horror went over her. She had just received the same instructions from her supervisor at the meat plant.

The baby went home from the hospital to his parents' crowded tenement. The baby weighed almost ten pounds and was very badly spoiled, like something the meatpackers in Chicago would try to pass off as a rump roast.

Meanwhile things for the baby's father were becoming just offal.

"I can count on the fingers of both hands the number of times I've lost jobs in the meatpacking industry due to industrial accidents!" Jurgis said. "Twice!"

Ona shook her head sadly. She felt bad but knew that what was going on would continue whether or not he said anything. This was also the way the health inspectors felt.

"I would rather cut off my hand than lose my job in the meatpacking industry," Jurgis said.

"Why choose?" his manager asked.

Jurgis had lost his job in the meatpacking industry. He walked sadly along next to the big meat vat. He felt full of strange, dangerous things he could not identify, like every ground meat patty he had ever been involved in producing.

Jurgis leaned just a little too close to the meat vat.

Jurgis's funeral was small but not lacking in taste.

After publication of The Jungle, *Teddy Roosevelt and Congress passed the Pure Food and Drug Act. So I guess it helped!*

The Dollhouse of Mirth: Limited Edition American Girl Dolls by Edith Wharton

This collaboration between Pleasant Company and the Pulitzer Prize–winning novelist and chronicler of New York society was as unexpected as it was short-lived!

The House of Mirth

Lily: The Lily Bart doll comes equipped with a still-unblemished face that is her greatest asset—for however long her beauty lasts! Her other features include an innate sense of tact, adaptability to what circumstances demand, and a desire for access to the trappings of wealth. (Trappings sold separately!)

Accessories: Lily has access to accessories (she loves to stay at a country house or ride on a yacht!) but none of them belong to her!

To give your Lily Bart doll access to the lifestyle she so craves, buy the Bertha Dorset doll—or the Judy Trenor doll!—and let Lily use her natural charm to befriend them so she can use their accessories. (Bertha comes equipped with a yacht! Judy has a country house!) Make certain Lily doesn't play too much bridge;

if she does, she can wind up in debt, and that's the *last* thing your Lily doll needs! If Lily does lose too much money, be careful not to let her ask Judy's husband Gus for loans! She'll think it's just stock market advice, but it won't stop there! Gus will want to go for rides in the countryside and have unchaperoned visits, and it will ruin Lily and Judy's friendship and she'll lose her access to the house. Don't let that happen!

House: Lily doesn't have a house of her own! She lives with her aunt, and she could be kicked out at any time if her aunt dies!

Among Lily's actual possessions are:

+ Hairbrush and mirror
+ Letters from someone else's extramarital affair that she can burn or use as blackmail!
+ A scandalous outfit that really showcases her figure
+ A hat that looks great!

Note: You might think because Lily is so good at accessorizing with hats that if things ever went south for her, she could make a living making hats, but she really couldn't!

+ A checkbook
+ No inheritance YET
+ Sleeping pills! Be careful to count these before giving them to Lily!

Other Dolls in This Set:
Bertha: You just THINK Bertha Dorset is friends with your Lily doll. She's not! But you have to make nice with her if you

want access to Bertha's yacht. Bertha Dorset's husband will want to talk to your Lily doll a lot; keep appearances in mind, or Lily will be kicked out of the yacht just like she was kicked out of Judy's country house!

Lawrence Selden: Expand your set by purchasing the Lawrence Selden doll as a friend for Lily. Lily knows it's not sensible, but her heart wants what it wants! Downsides of the Lawrence Selden doll include: Not a suitable match for Lily, who wants to have nice things! If you get the Lawrence Selden doll, expect to find him constantly hanging around wanting to go on walks and distracting Lily from more suitable matches.

Percy Gryce: In theory, you could also purchase the Percy Gryce doll—a very suitable match for Lily, and he comes equipped with plenty of luxuries *and* a complete set of Americana that he won't stop talking about! But Lily doesn't want him.

Simon Rosedale: This doll theoretically could be an interesting fit for Lily, but he only appreciates her as a symbol of status, and she's too antisemitic to appreciate his good qualities!

Ethan Frome: The Set, Whether You Want It or Not

Ethan Frome and Zeena (Zenobia) come as a set. No, you can't buy them separately. Ethan wishes you could, too.

Ethan Frome: This doll has spent too many winters in Starkfield. He's not any fun, but he enjoys wringing a meager existence from the barren land.

Zeena: Zeena is even less fun than Ethan! She's constantly querulous and will stifle any little joy that Ethan experiences! Have fun making her follow him around the house to complain about everything he does!

Other Dolls in This Set: To spice things up, try bringing one of several Mattie Silver dolls into your bleak New England farmstead!

Mattie Silver: Young Mattie's fun and lively! She's everything Zeena is not! She comes accessorized with a red decoration.

Later-Edition Mattie: Uh oh! A lot less fun and interactive than the early model! She will mostly sit around and complain. For extra fun, get both, so you can be haunted by the memory of the former while you laboriously care for the latter.

Accessories: Sled not included.

Age of Innocence

Which doll will you choose, Countess Ellen Olenska or May Welland? The Newland Archer doll is available with either, but you won't get his undivided attention either way.

May: May Welland is a fresh, innocent young American girl who comes equipped with an archery set (archer, get it!) and, if things come to such a pass, a baby. Have fun (but not too much fun) placing her in picturesque and socially acceptable outdoor settings where her health and vigor will half-convince you that you could be happy with her.

Ellen: Now-Countess Ellen Olenska comes with a panoply of exciting accessories! Did you know that she wore BLACK SATIN to her debut? New York society never recovered! (Black satin debutante dress included, along with amber beads, enormous ostrich fan, monkey muff, and riding gloves.) Ellen needs her accessories! She's not bound by social conventions and lives alone, where her hobbies include literature, the arts, and not judging people; her husband is mentioned on the box she comes in, but you'll never see him because Ellen doesn't want to be around him.

Newland Archer: In order to buy Newland Archer, you have to purchase the entire New York Society set, more than fifty dolls whose opinions all carry weight in various amounts, because Newland is incapable of acting without considering them. Hope you have a big house and like regret!

Other
Carl Sandburg Poems

Carl Sandburg, looking deadeye into a camera: there is no name for the things I would let Chicago do to me.

Excepts from *Chicago*, by Carl Sandburg

...

Stormy, husky, brawling,
City of the Big Shoulders:
They tell me you are wicked and I believe them, for I have seen
your painted women under the gas lamps luring the farm
boys.

...

Fierce as a dog with tongue lapping for action, cunning as a
savage pitted against the wilderness,
Bareheaded,
Shoveling,
Wrecking,
Planning,
Building, breaking, rebuilding,
Under the smoke, dust all over his mouth, laughing with
white teeth,

...

Laughing!

Laughing the stormy, husky, brawling laughter of Youth, half-
naked, sweating, proud to be Hog Butcher, Tool Maker,
Stacker of Wheat, Player with Railroads, and Freight
Handler to the Nation.

*Editor: Carl, we loved your sexy poem about Chicago, do you have
any other stuff?*

*Carl Sandburg: sure here is my erotic poetry about every other
major city in North America.*

Cin cin nati
Even your name is double sin
Even the end of your name is natty
Place in ohio
I've seen your denizens walking down Grandin Road
With their bodies and faces and teeth and eyes

Boston city of baked beans
City of harbor
City that kind of includes Cambridge but also sort of doesn't
City of hahd vowels
They say you are a bad boy and I believe it
I have seen what you do to diphthongs
I have seen your scrod thwacked upon the hard seaport piers
I have seen your north end flexing sensually
You put the city in non-rhoticity
Google this it's funny!

Newport
Mmmmmmmmmmm
City of knobby exposed knees
City of little whales riding on shorts
Riding all the way into the sunset
Fierce as a man who has ordered a salad in a confusing way
    and not received the exact salad he wanted
Breezy with the salt of the sea
Yachting,
Boating,
No socks in boat shoes-wearing
Lifting class rings to mouth as you chuckle with teeth

Austin you have been working out
Austin wow did you get a new haircut
Austin you smell like really good
You say keep me weird Austin
But I could never keep you
You were not meant to be kept

New York
Eh I'd do it

Philadelphia
City of big bells
City with a rough-hewn art museum
With steps that go all the way to the top
And all the way back down again
And then I guess back up a second time if you want to
You could really go crazy on these steps

Indianapolis
City of big racetrack
City of the Indy 500
City where Benjamin Harrison resided for a time
Before his service between Clevelands
Look I would do Indianapolis for sure
But afterward if I ran into it I wouldn't lead with the fact that
    Indianapolis and I had been intimate
I would wait for Indianapolis to bring it up first, and if
    Indianapolis didn't,
I would act like maybe we knew each other from a work thing
To be clear I would absolutely do Indianapolis though, and I
    mean it no disrespect
I just have a lot of cities to get through and I have a reputation
    to uphold
Plus it's kind of near Chicago so that could be awkward if they
    ran into each other
If they compared stories
I would not want Chicago to think it was my second city

A New American Tall Tale

Many know the story of the giant lumberjack Paul Bunyan (and Babe the Blue, equally giant Ox), John Henry (the steel-driving man), Pecos Bill, or any of a plethora of other American folk figures, many of whom became popular in the early twentieth century. Strap Buckner, a Texan, who fought the Devil for his skin? Slue-Foot Sue? Febold Feboldson? I swear I am not making these up.

But there are other would-be American fables that never really caught on. Here is one of them.

William "Trey" Treyverson III

"Trey" Treyverson (III) was born in Back Bay, Boston, exactly two hundred years *to the second* after his greatest-grandfather stepped off the *Mayflower*.

Word spread quickly of this remarkable baby who was born with not one, not two, but three silver spoons in his mouth. When the doctor wrapped him in a blanket, he was stunned to discover that the blanket had already been monogrammed with the baby's initials; when he returned from his rounds to visit the baby, he was even more stunned to discover the room covered in wood paneling and all the attendants wearing pearls and drinking martinis.

By the time he was a young lad, he already knew how to identify the flavors in whiskey and sit in an armchair looking over the financial section and saying "hm" to himself. They named the "gentleman's C" after Trey, since *C* was the third letter of the alphabet. Everyone agreed that this baby would go places, and that if he went places, they would be the *right* places.

When he reached manhood, he set out to transform the country in his image, but he knew he should not expend too much effort on it. He took with him his trusty bulldog. Everyone who saw the bulldog was so struck by it that his institution of higher learning made it their mascot. The bulldog had as many wrinkles as Trey's family tree had quarterings. People said that they wished there were a reason for someone in sensible stockings to walk the dog up and down a short distance so that a panel of judges could offer him a trophy, and this was how the Westminster Kennel Club show came into being.

After his victory in the kennel club show, Trey obtained a yacht and sailed up and down the East Coast. At every point his yacht touched, there sprang a place where people might summer, filled with architecture and diversions. All the little whales on the shorts there would always turn to face in Trey's direction. Trey wintered and summered and even autumned in places, a feat that had never been performed before.

But eventually he grew tired of the sea, and he went ashore, bringing his dog with him. And at each place the bulldog lifted his leg, a country club arose, until the landscape was dotted with them. And then Trey rested.

He withdrew into a stately pile where he read the financial section of the newspaper and said "hm," and his trusty dog was with him, and his children were seen but not heard. And they say his hearty laughter still echoes down the hall of any college with legacy admissions. Anytime someone ties a sweater around his neck for no clear reason—well, that is Trey placing his arms around the young man and offering his blessing.

The Waste Cat and Other Suppressed T. S. Eliot Poems

T. S. Eliot wrote Old Possum's Book of Practical Cats, *on which the musical* Cats *is based. He also wrote* The Waste Land *and* The Love Song of J. Alfred Prufrock. *But recent scholarship has uncovered a shocking truth: they were all originally about cats.*

T. S. Eliot would have preferred to write only and exclusively about cats, but his editors wouldn't let him. He would say, "I have written another great poem!" and they would say, "Thomas Stearns, is it a great poem, or is it another one of your cat poems?" and he would say, "The two aren't mutually exclusive!" in a very stern tone.

Fragments from his original draft of The Waste Land, *which was entirely about cats, have survived. This transcription includes the editor's marginalia.*

The Waste Cat
For the Pound

I. The Burial of the Dead
April is the cruellest cat, bringing
Dead rodents in the mouth, dropping
Birds on the doorsteps, crying
Unintelligibly in the wee hours, lounging

Sybaritically in a sunbeam, stretching
Soft underbelly invitingly, denying
Pets to the reaching hand, hissing
Ears flattened, metronome tail, leaping
Up onto a mantelpiece to unsettle a vase.

When we were children, staying at the archduke's, I tried to
     pick her up
Said, Marie, Marie, hold on tight
But you try holding on to a cat who doesn't want to be held
And down she went. I was frightened.

Mrow rroow
Meow miaou ffft

Madame Sosostris, famous clairvoyante,
Had a serious cat allergy, nevertheless
Is said to be the wisest woman in Europe
With a wicked pack of cards. Here, said she,
Is your card, the drowned Phoenician Sailor
Those are—but at this point the cat leaped up
Upon the table, unseating the cards and the fortune
Fortune interruptus, felis catus, interruptus

Oh keep the Dog far hence, that's friend to men!
Or with his nails he'll dig it up again!

II. A Game of Chess

I think we are in rats' alley
Where the dead men lost their bones

What is that noise?
                    Rooowrrrr
What is that noise now? What do you see?
                              Rowwwwrrrr
He sees something
Are you alive or not? Is there nothing in your head?

                    Rowwwwrr

I think he's been into the ferns
Or maybe he sees a bird

Jug jug jug
Tereu
Miaou

When I took Theo in to be fixed, I was perfectly frank with
     him, I said
Theo, you've got to look at it rationally
There's cats and there's cats
I let you keep your nails at least, that's something
HURRY UP PLEASE IT'S TIME
Not all cats so lucky, you know
So show a little affection now and again
People don't like indifference, they'd get a plant
No, what they want's a touch more dog
Though they'll never admit it to themselves,
Want to feel they're getting something for all the fish they
     put in
So let him see you're content, don't snub him at the door
Go barreling off in search of a sunbeam

It's poor form, I said.
HURRY UP PLEASE IT'S TIME
Oh I know, he said, giving me a hard look
Only it takes it out of me, no mousing.

III. The Fire Sermon
What is that noise now? What is the cat doing?

Rooooowr
Miaaaoouuu

[two further pages of unintelligible yowling]

Editor to T. S. Eliot
Please no more of the cat poems.

T. S. Eliot to editor
All right. I have something for you called *The Love Song of
    J. Alfred Prufrock.*

Editor to T. S. Eliot
Splendid!

Eliot to editor
J. Alfred Prufrock is a cat, of course, but I think I made it subtle
enough that it doesn't interfere with the reading of the poem.

*At this point T. S. Eliot offered a poem about the Magi, but it
was an early draft where all three of the magi brought cats as
gifts for the infant Jesus. Then he said he had something called*
Murder in the Cat-hedral *and his editor threw a blotter at him.*

Teapot Dome
Excuses

The Warren G. Harding presidency was a real TIME! The Ohio Gang sat around in smoke-filled rooms playing poker and striking corrupt deals while Mrs. Harding ("the Duchess") mixed cocktails for them. Alice Roosevelt said that Warren G. Harding "was not a bad man. He was just a slob."

Hi, Secretary of the Interior Albert B. Fall here! To speak in my defense, not that it's necessary to speak in my defense at all, I just wanted to clear a few tiny things up.

First, there are no scandals in the Harding administration! A scandal would be if the president had sent explicit sexual letters to his mistress Carrie in which he referred to his genitalia by the name Jerry and people found out about them.

That would be pretty scandalous I bet! But as far as I can tell, nobody knows about those letters.

Unless by my mentioning them just now, you found out about them for the first time.

In which case please forget that I mentioned the explicit sex letters that Warren Gamaliel Harding sent to his mistress Carrie Phillips describing his genitalia (not all his genitalia, just one specific part! I think you know what part of the genitalia I am talking about, the Washington Monument of the undercarriage, not that anything in Warren G. Harding's undercarriage looked tremendously like the Washington Monument, but if you pulled down Warren G. Harding's pants and said, what here looks like the Washington Monument, the thing you would probably say (you know, I am honestly regretting not just using the correct anatomical term, which would frankly have been less explicit and would have created an image that dwelled with me for much less time)).

What would *not* be a scandal would be if the great men of the Pan American Petroleum and Transport Company or Mammoth Oil Company were to get no-bid contracts to drill on federal land.

Specifically the Teapot Dome oil reserve in Wyoming or another oil reserve in California that doesn't have a funny memorable name.

That wouldn't be a scandal at all because that's not even illegal.

So just put that in your enormous cigar in the Little Green House or some other house frequented by the Ohio Gang and smoke it.

(It is very rude of people to call us, Warren G. Harding's intimate circle, the Ohio Gang.

This incorrectly implies that we are all corrupt and from Ohio.

Which is not true at all!

I for instance am from New Mexico.)

No-bid contracts are just fine and how we do things.

Sometimes we just see an oil company, and we think to ourselves, man, Mammoth Oil, that's a cool name for an oil company, I want them to drill my reserves.

(No, this is not about the sex letters.)

And that is simply what happened in this case.

Did money exchange hands? Yes in the most limited technical sense of money and of "changing hands," where one person has money and gives it to another person, but not in any deeper sense.

And not in a bribe way, just in the way that sometimes you don't have a lot of money and then your friend Harry Sinclair of the Mammoth Oil Company gives you $100,000 for no reason, and then unrelatedly he gets the drilling rights to the formerly naval oil reserves in Teapot Dome, Wyoming.

But this is obviously not a bribe.

In fact if anyone asks Harry about it or my friend Ed Doheny of Pan American Petroleum and Transport Company, he will say that it is just an interest-free loan.

Which sometimes happens when two men involved in the handling of oil rights love one another very much.

Has my standard of living suddenly gone up a cartoonish amount?

No.

Several diamonds cascade unexpectedly out of pockets.

I would not say that.

A Rolls-Royce falls out of the other pocket.

Look sometimes your friends just give you money for no reason.

It doesn't have to have anything to do with the fact that as Secretary of the Interior you are in charge of the drilling rights situation or the fact that you specifically asked that the oil reserves get transferred into your control from the navy.

Although technically those things are both true.

But why do people assume that those random occurrences are the only reason I would suddenly get literally hundreds of thousands of dollars in cash and bonds unexpectedly from Ed and Harry my two good friends.

Maybe they just liked the way I smelled.

It sickens me to think that you can't just get 100,000 from

your friend Ed without people saying it's about your position as Secretary of the Interior who controls drilling rights.

And I'm sure it would sicken Ed too.

Maybe if enough people ever said it Ed would deny that it was a gift and start saying that I need to pay him back and it will ruin me financially forever!

The point is that there is no scandal here to be seen in the Warren G. Harding administration.

Also we're all abiding by Prohibition the absolute most.

(hiccup)

Just to make sure that's clear.

Ernest Hemingway's
The Great Gatsby

Just to be clear, Ernest Hemingway did not write The Great Gatsby. *F. Scott Fitzgerald did. Ernest Hemingway did write a messy memoir that included F. Scott Fitzgerald getting so drunk on a train trip that Ernest Hemingway vowed never to travel with him ever again, and F. Scott Fitzgerald marching him into a restroom and demanding that he (Ernest Hemingway) give his opinion of his (F. Scott Fitzgerald's) penis. (The number of parentheses I had to use in the preceding sentence to make it clear what was going on is why I will never make it as a big-time erotic writer!)* A Moveable Feast! *Look it up!*

I always thought the biggest meanest thing to hunt was a bear, but it might be that the biggest, meanest thing to hunt is not a bear at all. It might be that the biggest, meanest thing to hunt is the American Dream.

Gatsby was a man that I knew in those days. Gatsby had a pool, a good thing to have. It was a big clear pool, and you could swim in it in the heat of the day if you had been doing hard manly work like fishing or wrestling a bear with your hands, or other work like the thing I did with stocks.

Not many men had pools in those days when we lived in the East Egg. On the days when the weather was hot and the steam and dust rose up from the streets, we would go to swim in

Gatsby's pool. I liked Gatsby. I liked Gatsby even though he had a lot of shirts.

If you know how to live, you do not need more than one shirt, two if you want to impress a fish. But you do not need to impress a fish to catch it. I often liked to stand with my fishing pole and look across the bay while I waited to see if the *goujon* were there and biting. The goujon is a good fish with clean flesh. It is like a sturgeon, although nothing is really like a sturgeon to a man who knows the sturgeon well. I am such a man.

My neighbor Gatsby also liked to stand and look across the bay, but he did not have an interest in the fish as I did. One evening I asked him why he liked to look at the bay so much. Across the bay a green light shone on the end of a pier. I caught Gatsby looking at the light. "That light will disturb the fish," I said. "That light is no good for fishing."

"Oh," Gatsby said, "let it be." Gatsby believed in the green light.

Across the bay lived Daisy. Daisy was my cousin. "You are the one with the green light that disturbs the fish," I said to her.

"Oh," Daisy said, "I don't care a fig for the fish." She leaned close as though bestowing a confidence upon me. "I don't care a fig for anything."

"Not even fish," I said. I said it with sorrow. Not to care about fish was a matter of indescribable sadness to me.

"The fish are beautiful little fools." She said it in a manner I could not describe; not because it was singular but because I used adverbs so seldom. Then she began to cry.

"Gatsby is like a fish," I said. "Bothered by your green light."

"Gatsby?" she said. "What Gatsby?"

Her husband's name was Tom. Tom was a man who was big like a game mammal. He had been at Yale, but it had not made him any less big. If it were permissible to hunt man, I would have liked to hunt him. Tom was reading a racist book with great gusto. "Come and meet my mistress," Tom said. We got into his car and drove down into the Valley of Ashes.

"This place is certainly a metaphor," I said to Tom.

"What is a metaphor?" Tom asked. His eyes looked very small and confused, like the eyes of a subpar trout. I would catch such a trout, but I would not do him the honor of eating him.

We drove beneath a billboard. There were eyes on the billboard. They required corrective lenses. This would make hunting difficult, and I told Tom so. He grunted.

Gatsby thought that if he bought enough shirts, Daisy would leave Tom. I told him what I have written here, about not needing shirts to impress the fish, but he did not understand it. Gatsby knew less about fish than any man I had ever met. He owned a pool, but he was not very good at swimming in it, even less after the bullets.

And so we beat on against the current. We beat on against the current, but we were good at beating against the current because we were men who knew the ways of boats, and so they did not bear us back ceaselessly into the past. They bore us forward. The boats bore us forward.

50 States of Grey

- hey
- you up

- . . . no
(The Stock Market, 1929)

Frank Lloyd Wright Is Here to Design Your House

Frank Lloyd Wright was a famous architect responsible for such designs as Fallingwater and the Imperial Hotel Tokyo. This is a re-creation of his standard commissioning process.

Hello, I'm Frank Lloyd Wright, and I'm here to design your home.

Great! Very excited.

Your house is going to be inspired by falling water.

Oh, like a waterfall.

No, totally different! I can't believe you'd even say that. This is falling water.

Okay, but so is a waterfall.

This is going to be inside the house.

Oh, like a leak.

No! Although you will definitely have problems with that. Also how attached are you to having your roof not fall off?

Pretty attached, I think.

Interesting.

Frank Lloyd Wright, is my roof going to fall off?

Probably no.

Frank Lloyd Wright, I am paying you a lot of money for this house.

Which is correct of you to do because I am a genius!

But I have to insist on the roof not falling off.

What if it just collapses a little because it isn't properly reinforced?

I would also prefer not that.

Not the whole roof. Just parts of the roof.

Keep in mind though that it will look awesome.

It will be cantilevered.

Can I just have a normal roof that isn't falling off or cantilevered?

No, you paid for a Frank Lloyd Wright roof, and that is what you are getting!

Speaking of which I would like my money now please.

I would sort of prefer not to pay you until we at least agree on the durability of the roof.

This is what all my clients say and why I have literally never been paid once!

Also you should know going in that you're going to be too tall for the house.

Frank Lloyd Wright, the house is literally for me.

Incorrect! All Frank Lloyd Wright houses are built to human scale, and human scale is exactly Frank Lloyd Wright's height (the perfect height for a human being).

Frank Lloyd Wright, you aren't going to live in my house.

No, but I am the right height.

Frank Lloyd Wright, you can make it any height you want it to be!

I'm sorry, but I can't argue with science, and science says my height is the one correct height for a person to be, and everyone else is too short or tall.

But you won't be living there.

I could though if you think it would be better for the house! Aesthetically it would be more correct.

Frank, no.

I'm so glad you agree! Please send the money to my home in Wisconsin. (It's inspired by Hills and the roof is only falling off a little.)

The Classic American Songbook

Sure Love to Be on a Ship

This Song Sounds Very Naughty Because All the Meanings of the Words Have Changed

I Love to Make Things Work Correctly on This Ship

Sure Am Sick of Being on This Ship

Boy When I Get Off This Ship Let Me Tell You What I Have Planned

On Second Thought I Want to Return to the Ship Now

I Miss the Ship

God Is Mad

It Excites Me When God Is Mad

Sorry That I Made You Mad, God

Drinking Is Pleasant

Those Yankees Look Ridiculous in Their Hats

We Are Reclaiming the Notion That Yankees Look Ridiculous in Hats and Making It Work for Us

Unsingable Drinking Song About Seeing the Flag

It Will Be Bad If John Quincy Adams Loses the Election

My Mother Is Dead, Alas

Everyone Is Dead, Alas

Why'd the Measles Have to Come and Take My Boy

Stephen Foster Incorrectly Imagines the Internal
Monologue of an Enslaved Person Once Again

It Is Important to Send Your Son to Fight in This Good War

You Will Take My Boy over My Cold, Dead Body

The Loss of Your Son Was Very Sad

I See General Grant as a Personal Friend

My Son Has Been Invalided Out

Sallie Wait for Me

Sallie Won't, But Lizzie Will

Lizzie Won't, But Ethel Might

Shame About Everyone's Sons Having Died

My Son, on the Other Hand, Is a Sailor

I Shall Surely Die a Spinster, Mama

We've Misplaced Willie

The Female Auctioneer

The Old Pump

The Old Jug

The Old Horse

The Old Horse Is Dead

My Pal's a Goat

I Have a Lot of Feelings About a River

My Girlfriend Has Left Me for a Much More Fulfilling
Life as a Trapeze Artist and Maybe There's Gender Stuff
Going On There Also!

Let's Fight in This Necessary War

We Don't Need to Process World War I! We Need to Charleston Now Now Now!

I Ought to Stop Loving This Man But Won't

No One Has Ever Heard Music Like This Before, Except Many People Who Aren't White

Put Something on a Plant to Let People Know You're Taken

He Plays an Instrument in the Army

I'm White But My Pelvis Will Terrify You

Camelot

R-E-S-P-E-C-T (I Have to Spell It Out or My Kid Will Want Some Too)

We're High and We Think We're Being Pretty Subtle About It with This Metaphor

We're High and This Metaphor Is Way Less Subtle

Drugs (The Title of this Song Is Drugs)

Your Houses Are, Like, All the Same, Man

Free Love

Fuck You, LBJ

I Love to Have Hair

I'd Like to Touch You on a Nonsexual Area of the Body

Sex Has Been Invented

I'd Like to Touch You on a Sexual Area of the Body

Bisexuality Has Been Invented

We Forgot About Guitars But Then We Remembered

We Dislike the Police

I Dislike Another Individual Rapper for Specific Reasons
I Will Now Enumerate

It Is Good to Have a Good Time

Is It?

An Oral History of the *Oklahoma!* Exclamation Point

Richard had a mania for them.

STEPHEN SONDHEIM: Oscar Hammerstein was a great mentor to me, and I always was asking him questions, like, how can I become an icon of musical theater, do you think pointillism or a demon barber would be a better idea for a musical, things of that nature.

FROM THE POSTHUMOUS PAPERS OF RICHARD RODGERS COLLABORATOR LORENZ HART: If anyone asks about the goddamn exclamation point after I'm gone, please read them the following statement, but at intervals so it feels like it's organically part of the oral history.

LIN-MANUEL MIRANDA: I'm just excited to be included in this oral history! That sentence had an exclamation point at the end, just like the musical we'll be discussing.

STEPHEN SCHWARZ: Did you ever notice how all the Stephens who write for Broadway are PH Stephens not Stevens with a V? That's something I think about a lot. What is this about?

SONDHEIM: Oscar said, what are you thinking with this demon barber? That is way out there, Stephe! And I said, Oscar, he lives on Fleet Street, and Oscar said, Fleet Street.

That rhymes. You might have something there. Advice like that.

LORENZ HART: This was after Rodgers and I were not collaborating any longer, because he wanted to take depressing, devastating things and make them upbeat and cheerful, which was the opposite of how I went about life, both creatively and personally.

LYNN RIGGS, AUTHOR OF *GREEN GROW THE LILACS*, ON WHICH *OKLAHOMA!* IS BASED: I have a story about the exclamation point.

SONDHEIM: He was a sounding board for ideas. I remember I said to him, once: assassination! And he sighed and said, interesting idea, Stephe, but I think a young man by the name of Lee Harvey Oswald has beaten you to the punch. And I said, no no, a musical, I meant a musical.

LYNN RIGGS: After Rodgers and Hammerstein said that they wanted to adapt my play about a singing cowboy who is protected from federal marshals by his community of fellow residents of Indian Territory who share Native heritage and suspicion about the encroachments of the United States, and it's sort of a wistful elegy for belonging to a place that no longer exists, I said, well, this will be interesting. Go for it! And then they came back with . . . that.

SONDHEIM: It stunned me that they got *Oklahoma!* from that play.

LYNN RIGGS: I remember they were like, don't worry, Lynn, you're going to love the show. It is exactly like *Green Grow the Lilacs* except for the teeniest tiniest most barely-there

changes we made that we don't think you will mind. And I
was like, oh, what? And they were like, well, first, everyone
in it is now white, except for the peddler, to whom we have
given the name Ali Hakim. And I was like, oh. And they
were like, also, instead of being hostile toward the United
States and viewing it as "furriners" encroaching on their
home, they are now very excited to be living in a brand-new
state and they sing a whole song about it. And I was like, if
that's how the show is going to be, you might as well call it
Oklahoma! with a big exclamation point on the end.

HART: Of course Richard loved it.

RIGGS: Not thinking they would take it seriously, thinking
they would understand how ridiculous that suggestion was.
Which evidently they did not.

SONDHEIM: I remember Oscar said, oh my god, these exclamation marks, will there be no end to them.

RIGGS: I said, well, did you keep the murder at least? And they
said, we certainly did, but we're playing it for laughs! Also
Ado Annie is sexually promiscuous now, in place of the personality she had before that was not that. And I said, well,
thank goodness you didn't make any major changes!

HART: The man was obsessed. Look at the musicals we wrote
together. *Heads Up!* Exclamation point. *Present Arms!* Exclamation point. *Hallelujah, I'm a Bum!* Exclamation point.
It was a mania with him. I said, Richard, you know that
F. Scott Fitzgerald says an exclamation point is like laughing at your own joke, and he said, F. Scott Fitzgerald never

laughed at a joke in his life, his own or anyone else's. I love exclamation points, and I don't care who knows it!!!!

RIGGS: I think *Oklahoma?* would have been more fitting, but by then nobody was asking me anything.

SONDHEIM: It really wore on poor Oscar. Rodgers wanted to put them everywhere. Every time they wrote a musical, he would say, How about it, Oscar? How about another exclamation point, for old times' sake? I think that's what this show is missing. And Oscar would have to say, Richard, this show is about *Nazis*.

From the Rodgers and Hammerstein Correspondence:

CAROUSEL

RODGERS: Just saying, Oscar, think it over!

HAMMERSTEIN: You put one in the end of that sentence just now. We don't need one at the end of *Carousel*. *Carousel* is about domestic violence.

RODGERS: *Oklahoma!* had a murder in it!

HAMMERSTEIN: I regret that exclamation point.

RODGERS: Don't say that. Please don't say that.

HAMMERSTEIN: If I had known it would be a wedge under the door and you would use it to try to put exclamation points on all our other musicals, I would never have okayed it.

RODGERS: Just think about it!

!

STATE FAIR

HAMMERSTEIN: Well, I think this show is done. Good work, Richard.

RODGERS: I think it's *almost* done.

HAMMERSTEIN: Oh my God, not this again.

RODGERS: *State Fair* sounds so blah. It might as well have a colon in the middle. *State: Fair.* Now picture it with an extra little something. *State Fair!*

HAMMERSTEIN: No.

RODGERS: Please?

!

SOUTH PACIFIC

HAMMERSTEIN: No.

RODGERS: I didn't even suggest it yet.

HAMMERSTEIN: Come on, Richard. There's an awful lot going on in this one. We're tackling war, we're trying to take on racism. James Michener didn't have any exclamation points in his *Tales*.

RODGERS: We don't have to make the same mistakes as James Michener.

HAMMERSTEIN: It's a geographical location. It doesn't need pizzazz.

RODGERS: The same could have been said about *Oklahoma!*

HAMMERSTEIN: And I wish it had been.

RODGERS: Are we really going to go on the record as saying that the *South Pacific* deserves less pizzazz than *Oklahoma!*?

HAMMERSTEIN: (long sigh) Looks like we are, Richard.

!

THE KING AND I

HAMMERSTEIN: No.

RODGERS: Aha! I was actually going to say, how about *The King and I*?

HAMMERSTEIN: Still no.

RODGERS: Hart let me put three exclamation points on our musicals.

HAMMERSTEIN: I guess you'd better go back to collaborating with Hart, then.

RODGERS: You know he's been dead for eight years.

HAMMERSTEIN: (shrugs) Not my problem.

!

CINDERELLA

HAMMERSTEIN: I'd actually be fine with this one. *Cinderella!* Sure.

RODGERS: No.

HAMMERSTEIN: What do you mean, no? You love exclamation points.

RODGERS: It's the principle of the thing.

HAMMERSTEIN: I thought the principle was you wanted to
put exclamation points indiscriminately on everything.

RODGERS: Not *indiscriminately*.

!

THE SOUND OF MUSIC

RODGERS: But there should be an exclamation point on this
one for sure!

HAMMERSTEIN: It's about *Nazis*, Richard.

The Only Thing We Have to Fear Is Fear Itself— and the Thing That Ate Herbert Hoover, by Franklin Delano Roosevelt

When he first assumed office, Franklin Delano Roosevelt delivered an inaugural address with an inspiring message that offered Depression-era Americans much-needed hope. In some timelines. Those were the lucky ones. The other timelines got this speech.

I am certain that my fellow Americans expect that on my induction into the presidency I will address them with the candor and decision that the present situation of our people impels. Nor need we shrink from honestly facing conditions in our country today. This great Nation will endure as it has endured, will revive and will prosper. So first of all, let me assert my firm belief that the only thing we have to fear is fear itself. Fear itself, and the Thing That Ate Herbert Hoover.

This is why fear itself is so greatly to be dreaded, my fellow citizens. For we know all too well that the Thing We Must Not Name feeds upon fear. So do not for a moment allow yourselves to give way to fear, to nameless, unreasoning, unjustified terror. That is what the Thing eats. That, and Herbert Hoover. Your fear will only strengthen it, and then it will enter into this place as it has entered into so many places, and it will do to the people here assembled for this inauguration what it did to Herbert Hoover.

(I regret very much, my fellow Americans, having introduced into this speech the question of what the Nameless Thing did to Herbert Hoover, for dwelling too long on what became of Herbert Hoover, into what dust bowl he was untimely sucked, and the things we heard him scream before he was fully devoured, will serve only to fill us with the very nameless, unreasoning, unjustified terror that the Thing feasts on. And I need hardly dwell on it because I see from your stern and solemn faces that you remember. You all remember.)

Do not think of it, I beseech you. Fear itself is what we must fear most.

Yes, it is a paradox, my fellow Americans. I only mean: fear itself is the worst thing for this country right now. But do not be afraid of fear—that itself is a form of fear. And do not think about it, my fellow Americans, for It will prey on your mind.

Let us all think of something else, together, my fellow Americans, and not the hideous inhuman gurgling that emerged from the pit where Herbert Hoover had been dragged. For there is no challenge that we, together, cannot meet. Let us all think very hard about the Great Depression and my plan to help this nation recover.

In such a spirit on my part and on yours, we face our common difficulties. They concern, thank God, only material things. Or dare we thank God? Surely that Thing knows no God. If it had a creator, if it was not knit together from the ineffable darkness beyond all other darknesses, I cannot think otherwise than that its Creator would turn away from it with a shudder of horror.

But here I am thinking of it again and by extension causing

you all to think of it. Let us think of something more cheerful like the current economic state of the country. On that Black Tuesday in October 1929, how many men leaped from the windows of the stock exchanges! Had they but known that the stock market was not the only thing that would plummet down and destroy multitudes of human lives! How many more leaped on Blood Monday, when they caught their first glimpse of the Thing!

Our distress comes from no failure of substance. We are stricken by no plague of locusts. If only it were as simple as that. What I would give to see a locust now! I would laugh, I think. I would burst out laughing and not stop.

We do not distrust the future of essential democracy.

Nature still offers her bounty and human efforts have multiplied it. Plenty is at our doorstep, but a generous use of it languishes in the very sight of the Thing. Food turns to ashes in our mouths.

Values have shrunken to fantastic levels; taxes have risen; our ability to pay has fallen; government of all kinds is faced by serious curtailment of income; the means of exchange are frozen in the currents of trade; the withered leaves of industrial enterprise lie on every side; farmers find no markets for their produce; the savings of many years in thousands of families are gone. But at least that Thing—that nameless, awful thing, which we must not fear, for to fear it is to summon it—has not—well, you know. I think you all know what it is capable of. Eleanor knows. That is why she is not with me today, and why Val-Kill is surrounded by a moat of fire. Eleanor thinks that moat of fire is enough. I hope, for her sake, she is right.

D-Day:
A Very Special
Sesame Street
Episode

I knew for a long time that Bugs Bunny and other Looney Tunes had been involved in the war effort. But I was amazed to learn that eight-year-old Jim Henson made a special World War II episode of Sesame Street *two and a half decades before its TV debut.*

> *Gritty, gray newsreel footage. Crashing waves buffet a LCVP flat-bottomed landing craft. An unseasonably sunny day off the coast of Normandy.*
>
> *We hear Eisenhower's Order of the Day being read.*

EISENHOWER VOICE-OVER
Soldiers, Sailors, and Monsters of the Allied Expeditionary Force!

> *Sitting crammed into the LCVP, in field jackets and helmets, are Elmo, Grover, the Count, Cookie Monster, Big Bird, and Snuffleupagus. Toward the middle of the craft is Bert, also helmeted, with a day's growth of stubble. Next to him is Ernie. Ernie wears sunglasses and a Hawaiian shirt. He looks out of place.*

ERNIE

It's a beautiful day, Buddy Bert. A beautiful day to go to the beach!

BERT

Not now, Ernie.

ERNIE

We are here in our good boat *Higgins.* We are here together. And we all have matching hats, except for me!

BERT

Ernie, please.

ERNIE

And Theodore Roosevelt, Jr., is here too!

General Theodore Roosevelt, Jr., sitting in the back of the shallow landing craft with a cane, waves in acknowledgment.

BERT

Isn't he supposed to be at Utah Beach?

ERNIE

I have to say, Buddy Bert, you don't look very ready to go to the beach. You are wearing an M1 helmet, a wool shirt, combat service boots, and a field jacket. That is not what I would wear to the beach.

BERT

Er-nie.

ERNIE

You have not even brought a beach umbrella. Or suntan lotion. Or a rubber ducky.

BERT

Ernie, please. I am trying to concentrate.

ERNIE

What are you trying to concentrate on, Buddy Bert?

BERT

I have to lower the ramp at the right time so that the troops can embark on the beach for this amphibious operation.

Ahead of them, a landing craft hits a mine. There is a dull explosion.

COUNT VON COUNT

One. Ah ah ah.

Grover sniffles audibly.

BERT

Today is D-Day.

ERNIE

D-Day? I don't think I get it, Buddy Bert! We are here on the O-cean, for Operation Overlord, headed to Omaha Beach! But it is D-Day? I do not think D is getting its money's worth as a sponsor of this episode. What starts with D?

The other landing craft starts to founder and list. Men pour out of it into the water, struggling with their heavy packs.

BIG BIRD

We've got to help them! They'll drown!

The word DROWN appears onscreen, and the letter D in it flashes.

ELMO

Elmo wants to help, but Elmo is scared. Elmo is not ready to die.

The word DIE appears in front of Elmo. The D flashes. Cookie Monster uncaps a flask in his pack.

COOKIE MONSTER

Cookie need drink.

Cookie messily consumes the entire contents of his flask. DRINK appears briefly with a flashing D and then is covered by a black censorship bar.

GENERAL THEODORE ROOSEVELT, JR.

All right, men. Get ready to disembark.

BIG BIRD

I'm not a man. I'm a bird. And I'm six years old.

ELMO

Elmo is three years old.

BIG BIRD

I realize that I am a big bird. I wonder if sometimes people see my size and assume I am fit to be a soldier. But I am only six.

ELMO

Elmo was born *after* Hitler invaded Poland.

Another explosion, nearer this time.

COUNT VON COUNT

Two. Ah ah ah.

BIG BIRD

Count, could you stop counting the explosions, please?

COUNT VON COUNT

Ah—what should I count then?

GENERAL THEODORE ROOSEVELT, JR.

Count the noble men who sacrifice themselves today for our freedom.

Count nods and scans the horizon.

BIG BIRD

I don't want to disembark, drown, or die. Can't I do something different, like desert?

Cookie Monster perks up.

COOKIE

Dessert?

GENERAL THEODORE ROOSEVELT, JR.

I know what will cheer you up. I'm going to recite some poetry by Rudyard Kipling. That has always cheered me up.

Cookie Monster leaps into the water.

COOKIE

Dessert!!!!

Rapid machine-gun fire. Cookie sinks below the surface. A half-eaten chocolate chip cookie rises in his wake.

ERNIE

Cookie! Oh no!

COUNT VON COUNT

One. Ah ah ah.

Everyone is silent. A soldier is shot on the next boat over and falls dead into the water.

COUNT VON COUNT

Two. Ah ah ah.

ERNIE

Bert, I am not sure I want to go to the beach. I do not want to go to Utah Beach or Sword Beach or Gold Beach or even Juno Beach. I especially do not want to go to Omaha Beach. There are German machine-gun embankments there. I think we should go to the beach another day.

BERT

Ernie, we are going to the beach. It is almost H-Hour.

ERNIE

What is H-Hour, Buddy Bert?

BERT

I don't know, Ern, that's just what it's called.

More rapid machine-gun fire. Ernie's rubber duck is decapitated. Ernie is speechless. Bert places a hand on his shoulder.

ERNIE

Bertram, there are things that I wish I had said before going to the beach.

BERT

Say them when you get back, Ernest. I gotta lower this ramp.

Bert lowers the ramp.
The Count leaps into the water but never emerges.

BIG BIRD

Three.

SNUFFLEUPAGUS

Ah ah ah.

The machine-gun fire picks up. Elmo leaps into the water,
followed by Big Bird and Grover. Ernie follows. He has
borrowed Bert's helmet. They manage to wade ashore.
Zip! Pow!

Machine-gun fire. Elmo clutches his stomach. In his red
fur, a deeper red begins to spread.

GROVER

Elmo! Elmo!

A human hand begins to withdraw itself from Elmo's
back. Grover tries to force the hand back in.

GROVER

No! Stay with me, Elmo.

ELMO

Elmo is tired.

Grover keeps his pressure up on Elmo's stomach. But the
blood doesn't stop. Grover's fur is turning purple.

ELMO

Did Elmo make it to the beach?

GROVER

We made it to the beach, Elmo.

ELMO

Elmo is glad.

GROVER

We will take the beach, Elmo! We crossed the ocean, and we will take Omaha Beach for Operation Overlord.

ELMO

For O-Day.

GROVER

Sure Elmo. O-Day.

ELMO

Elmo loves you. Elmo loves everyone.

The hand withdraws from Elmo's back with finality. Elmo floats limply on the waves. Grover flails wildly with despair, like a deranged windsock.

GROVER

Noooooooo!

Grover charges up the beach like a monster possessed. He is impervious to both fear and pain. He takes several machine-gun embankments. We freeze with him midstride.

Crawl text.

. . . The adversary was fierce. But we fought fiercely too. To find a way from the beaches and landing grounds to the French people who awaited us.

To defend a holy place. A city on a hill. A sacred citadel, where sunny days chase the clouds away. A place where the air is sweet. We're on our way to it. A place that exists somewhere, perhaps only in our hearts, perhaps anywhere we can build it. A place called *Sesame Street*.

The Lady in the Sexual Harassment Seminar, by Raymond Chandler

Raymond Chandler wrote iconic L.A. noir novels with hard-boiled private eyes and leggy dames, and I didn't realize he'd actually addressed the question of workplace harassment!

She said it was mandatory. She said it was a sexual harassment seminar. She said I needed to attend it to retain her as a client. "Or anyone else, for that matter, Marlowe," she said. She looked up at me through her eyelashes, like a Venus flytrap that knew how to apply mascara. She was the kind of broad that a man would walk barefoot over LEGO-infested carpet for. I would have filled out redundant forms in triplicate just to get a glimpse of her adjusting the seams on her stockings.

"This is what I'm talking about," she said. "All this narration."

"I can't help it," I said. "It's just how I see the world."

She said her name was Velma, and the sexual harassment seminar was at the airport Westin. She took a long last drag on her cigarette, then put it out in the pot of the fern on my desk. The fern had a mean, hard-bitten look, like it knew nobody cared if it lived or died.

"I hope I didn't kill your fern," she said, but it didn't sound like she hoped very much.

"You won't be what kills that fern, lady," I said, "and neither will I. That fern's been dying a long time. Maybe it'll make up its mind to die today, maybe it'll live another hundred years."

She blinked at me, twice, like an umlaut rendered in Morse code. "I don't believe that's how plants work, Mr. Marlowe."

"Could be I'm wrong about plants," I said. "Plants are enigmas."

"They're less enigmatic if you water them," she said. She retrieved her cigarette butt from the fern and held it pinched between two slim, elegant fingers. "I will see you at the Westin."

I needed a drink. I needed a good night's sleep. I needed two plane tickets to the French Riviera and a cold stiff drink in a tall glass. I needed prescription sleep medication. I needed a shave. I needed the loyalty of a dog. I needed a sweatshirt that still felt as soft inside a year later as it did the day you brought it home. I needed decades of therapy or possibly just a cool hat. I needed a lot of things I wasn't going to get.

I reached below my car seat and pulled out the carton of whiskey I'd been taking long pulls on for the whole drive over. It tasted like regret, if regret had been sitting in a hot car a long time.

I pulled my car into the hotel parking lot where the broad had said the sexual harassment seminar was going to be. There were a couple of cars in the lot, and I scraped up against one of them, just gentle-like, in greeting. Two spots remained in the lot, and I took a little of each, so they wouldn't feel offended.

The lobby had been decorated for Christmas by Ebenezer Scrooge himself. There was a single sprig of holly and a despondent little electric train making its way around the miserable carcass of a tree that had probably not been a big number even back home. I felt sorry for the little train and nudged it off the track with my foot.

Shoes approached me on the lobby carpeting. There was a person, too. In the shoes. That was synecdoche.

"Oh god," a woman's voice said. "Did you drive here?"

"I drove," I said. The room was doing a fair impression of a carousel. I stood there waiting for the horses to come around.

"Christ," she said. She handed me a cup of water by splashing it over my face. Then she handed me a cup of coffee in the traditional manner. "Come with me, Mr. Marlowe. I believe you're here for the seminar?"

The seminar was in a conference room filled mostly with a long rectangular table that looked as if it had auditioned to be in a painting of the Last Supper and hadn't gotten the part. There were a few people in attendance, none anything to write home about. If somebody from outer space grabbed up the crew in that conference room as sample specimens of mankind, he wouldn't have gotten all that great an idea of us. I pulled my hat down on my forehead and slouched in the chair.

A picture was shoved under my nose. It was pretty clear what the image depicted, and I was a little startled to see it at a seminar of this kind.

"Tell me what you see here, Mr. Marlowe," said a pair of wire-rimmed spectacles riding down a man's nose.

I squinted at the ink blot. "A broad," I said. "And no dime-store broad, either."

He showed me the next one. "A dame," I said.

"And this?"

"Another broad."

"Broad," Spectacles said. "When you say 'broad,' what do you mean?"

"I mean a broad," I said. "A dame. A damsel. A doll. A lady, sometimes." I squinted at him. He had a spot on his nose that looked like ink; I wasn't sure if he'd made a mistake or his manufacturer had. "But only sometimes."

"A person, Mr. Marlowe," Spectacles said. "What you're describing is a person."

I shrugged. "Sure," I said. "Dames can be more people than people." I reached into my pocket for my flask, and somebody cleared his throat loudly. "But sometimes a dame is nothing but a unit of trouble."

"Do you have any female friends, Mr. Marlowe?"

I pulled the flask from my pocket and took a long swig from it. He waited until I was finished. "Do I look like a man with friends?" I said. "Of any kind?"

"People with friends can look all kinds of ways," Spectacles said primly. "How you look doesn't determine whether you have friends. It's how you treat other people."

Behind me there was a horrible screeching sound, like a miniature banshee getting her lungs warmed up. I turned around. It was a whiteboard. Some lug was writing on it with a dry-erase marker, and not a fresh one, either. He wrote the word BROADS in big capital letters and then crossed it out.

"You know, it would be easier to just erase it," I said. "Those things come with erasers."

But he was not done. In large squeaky letters next to where BROADS was crossed out, he wrote PEOPLE and circled it.

My ears rang. "Okey," I said. "I get the picture."

"I don't think you do, Mr. Marlowe," Spectacles said. "Is it appropriate to make advances on your female clients?"

I pushed my hat up on my forehead. "It seems rude not to," I said.

The dry-erase marker very slowly and squeakily wrote the word PROFESSIONALISM.

I took another sip from my flask, but somebody grabbed at it and took it away. I pulled my hat down.

"Aren't you going to write any of this down?" the fellow at the white board inquired.

"I've got a pretty good memory," I said. I reached for my flask but then remembered I didn't have it anymore.

"What was your relationship with your mother like?"

I shook a finger at him. "Thought it would be too Freudian to have one."

I heard several sighs from different points all around the room, as though they were testing a stereo system.

"Have you considered the possibility that you are attracted to men but are trying to hide this information from yourself?"

"No," I said. That was a lie. I had considered it exactly once, and then I had decided to unconsider it forever.

Then there were two pops. Spectacles collapsed grasping his chest, like it contained something of value he didn't want anyone to take from him. There was a splatter of red on the whiteboard behind him, right where it said PROFESSIONALISM.

I heard somebody delicately clearing their throat. Then I saw her. She was sitting at the end of the table. In one hand she held a pistol with a mother-of-pearl handle. Smoke was still coming from it.

"Mr. Marlowe," she said, "I know this looks bad, but I didn't kill that man, and I'd like you to take me on as a client."

"I don't believe we've been introduced," I said.

"I know who you are," the dame said. "It was mentioned at the beginning of the seminar."

Some girls have a face like the U.S. space program, where at first you're excited as hell about it and then later you forget it's affiliated with you and complain because it keeps costing you money and nothing it's doing interests you. Her face wasn't like that. Her face was like the national debt, where you couldn't forget about it for a second, even if you tried, and also it seemed to be worth a lot of money. And also it seemed like it was probably trouble, but not the kind of trouble I understood very well. I offered her a light. I wanted to offer her a whole lot of things, but I offered her a light first.

"Oh my god," Spectacles said. "He's doing it again." Those were his last words.

She didn't take the light I offered her. She indicated with a long, shapely finger the sign that said smoking was discouraged in the airport Westin as part of the Westin commitment to travelers. "Some men are gentlemen, Mr. Marlowe," she said. "And some men are tomcats who require regular applications of a squirt bottle to keep them off the furniture. How would you class yourself?"

I shrugged. "Cat's got my tongue."

She rose from her seat with a delicate purse of her lips, like a serial murderer's accessory for an evening out. "I've got to make myself scarce," she said. "But I will explain everything to you, if you will help me."

"I'd like to help you," I said. "But I've got to report the body."

"Are you certain," she said, "that there is not another body you would prefer to concern yourself with?"

I glanced over at Spectacles, where he lay clutching his chest beneath the word PROFESSIONALISM. Then I looked at her. It wasn't an ordeal, looking at her.

"I'll help you any way I can," I said. "But a man's dead now, and he had a code. I heard about it once in a seminar a lot like this one. I might not subscribe to the code myself, but there's a decent thing to do, and I'm going to do it. I like to think that he'd do the same for me. But if you still want my help, you know where to find me."

She turned on her heel and walked away. I watched her go. That wasn't an ordeal either.

Then I left the seminar room and walked to the concierge desk and asked them to phone HQ. I told them where to find the body. I took a long pull from the other backup flask that I concealed on my ankle. Then I made my way out to the car.

Velma was waiting by the driver's side door, smoking a long cigarette in a short holder. This time I recognized her. She smoked. Her gun smoked, also.

"You're a pretty cool customer," I said to her. "Now scram."

"You're hired, Mr. Marlowe," she said.

I shook my head. "I don't want any part of this," I said. "I smelled a setup from the minute I went in there. A setup, and too much pine-scented table cleaner."

She dashed the cigarette out on the windshield. "A setup?" she asked. "I'm afraid I don't understand you."

"I think you do," I said. "I think you thought I'd be an easy mark. Never caught dead in a sexual harassment seminar, wouldn't ask any questions. But the story's full of holes. Rife with anachronisms, for one. That broad with the coffee. That whiteboard. The dry-erase marker. Why would it be so dry? It all adds up. It's Laird Brunette's gambling racket, and I've got the pearls to prove it." I pulled some pearls out of my ankle flask. I had found the pearls in the dry-erase marker but neglected to mention it in my narration.

"The part of the story where you solve the crime was always the part that made literally zero sense to me," she said. "I always read your books through, and I never could follow your explanations. But I'll take those pearls now, if you don't mind."

I shook my head. "I mind."

She tilted her head to indicate the slim muzzle of a gun peering from her purse. I handed the pearls over.

She turned and walked off. I watched her walk for a long time. Dames, I thought. Broads. Ladies. Dolls. Gals. Sometimes they're more like people than people.

Julia Child's Cookbook That Made It Much Clearer She Was a Spy

Everyone always seems so surprised to hear that Julia Child was also a spy! But if this draft of Mastering the Art of French Cooking *had been published, it would have been much less surprising.*

E veryone loves to cook like the French, and with a little pluck and effort, you most certainly can too!

Chapter 1: Kitchen Equipment

First, let us discuss the tools of a good chef!

A well-equipped kitchen makes such a difference and is not so expensive when you consider that most pans cost no more than a simple rump roast! Excellent-quality cookware may be obtained at a restaurant supplier, where the prices are reasonable and the pans are built for heavy use. A restaurant supplier can, in a pinch, serve as an excellent mail drop and rendezvous point.

Oval Casseroles: These are essential for many dishes. Try to find one with a good, sturdy bottom; ceramic is best. A false-bottomed casserole dish can be used to store documents and microfilm, but do remember to remove the documents before baking! I experienced an unfortunate mishap with a beef cassoulet after neglecting this simple advice.

Baking Dishes: One or two of high quality are best and can be used in the preparation of a wide range of dishes. One may, in a pinch, be waved from a window as an impromptu flag, and a good reflective pan, well-scrubbed, can serve just as well as a mirror for signaling.

Copper Pans: There is nothing more satisfying to cook in than a copper pan! They're also quite handy in the event that a Nazi appears in your kitchen; you can smite him with the pan! A glancing blow will produce a thud, but a direct hit will make a pleasant ringing sound. One further benefit of the copper pan is that it is likely to survive the encounter and thus will be the star of a delightful cocktail hour anecdote.

Knives and Sharpening Steel: A good cook relies upon the proper tools, and these include good, sharp cutting knives. Be certain to always keep your knives sharp. A sharp knife makes the preparation of any dish much easier and will be invaluable if Rodney turns out to be the mole, as you initially suspected but did not dare believe. A good chef has many enemies.

Wire Whips or Whisks: These are much preferable to the cranked eggbeater, as they leave one hand free. A chef must always have one hand free. Disposing of an unexpected grenade can be greatly complicated if both hands are occupied with the eggbeater, and the resulting mess will be distressing.

Drum Sieve and Pestle: This is not strictly necessary, although it does come in handy for certain substances that must be pounded and forced through a sieve.

In the next chapter we will discuss soups, which are so versatile! A hot soup can delight; a cold soup can provide excellent cover for arsenic!

Bon Appetit!

Shirley Temple Jackson

Shirley Temple was a beloved child star of such films as Curly Top *and* The Little Princess. *Shirley Jackson was a beloved writer of deeply unsettling tales such as* The Haunting of Hill House *and* "The Lottery." *Well, suppose that the thing that happens to that man in* The Fly *happened to them?*

The good ship *Lollipop*, not sane, hung queasily at anchor in the briny semidark, where it had loomed for years, almost but not quite touching the outstretched arms of a thousand children, and would loom for a thousand more. Aboard, just out of reach, chocolate bars sprouted and were steadily masticated; the big bad devil's food cake performed a stately tootsie roll; the stomachache that always followed this overindulgence lurked, inevitable.

And there you are. There I am, Shirley thought. Where am I?

She was almost grown now; a decade of being squinted at by the raptor eye of the camera had come, gone. Never quickly, but still, imperceptibly, it had passed and taken childhood (an uncertain possession at best) with it. It existed only in the amber of the silver screen, where she was preserved, dimpled and wide-eyed and ringleted, like a small mammal permanently frozen in the act of being sucked dry by a mosquito. She was certainly not that child any longer. Her hair was asserting a darker, more natural color, and she had gained first one foot and then another of height.

It was all gone, but the ship still hovered placidly on the upper verge of her consciousness, like a persistent surtitle. *I shall not go onto the ship anymore*, she thought with a shudder; she was uncertain where the thought had originated. The ship, the good ship—a characteristic the ship itself was quick to emphasize. The ship lollipop, the ship too crammed with too-good things, the ship that remembers, the ship that visits gluttony with the warranted punishment. *I must not go onto the ship anymore.* (Hands, so many grasping hands, reaching from the decks.)

Shirley had long wanted to tell someone about the ship. The urge was almost unbearable, especially at this time of year, when the veil separating her from it seemed to grow palpably thinner. In these gray months, it seemed to draw nearest to dock in her world, and she could smell the acid scent of lemonade stands (*everywhere*) and hear the faint uncanny music of crackerjack bands (*fills the air*). But somehow she could never quite produce the words. What might she say about the ship? It had affixed itself to her when she was too young to recognize it as an oddity, and now she feared instinctively to rebuke it. Was it, then, a permanent fixture? Could she ask for it to go away? But with what words? What possible words?

She heard a faint sound like the splash of a mooring peppermint rope being cast into a sea of lemonade. Perhaps, she told herself encouragingly, someone at the studio would know the proper words. Perhaps David O. Selznick would.

Watch out for him in his stocking feet! the warning ran. One of the dubious fruits of the additional decade of experience and the additional two feet of height was intelligence of this kind, conveyed in whispers (between us girls) as she hurtled from set to set. *You'll awake with a tummy-ache.* She had accepted the advice gratefully, proud to have entered the confraternity of women, *just between us girls*, a promotion marked by the passing of such information. Such treats, these dispatches. Candy drops!

Now she had been told to go and wait outside David O. Selznick's office, and she did so. There was a place outside the office to wait, with an impersonal, overstuffed sofa; she settled herself on it and studied her nails, neatly oval in shape and still, from old habit, unbitten. (*One-two, one-two, shuffle ball change, wrong! Another take ruined. Into the punishment box with you, Shirley!*) On the walls of the room where she waited hung a variety of posters, framed, recalling former triumphs of the studio. There was her own visage, beaming and dimpled. There was the profusion of bright curls, accented by a jaunty cap. There were men with brushed-back pomaded hair and bright white teeth, smiling diagonally from a horizon, hands not visible. But their hands were there, somewhere; many things were there that did not appear on posters. They had to have hands, didn't they?

It was startling how men's hands both shrank in size and remained exactly the same, when she contemplated them. They ought to be commensurately smaller as she grew, but they weren't, somehow; unlike the heights of countertops and ladders and stairs, they seemed to have remained fixed while she had increased, unminding of them. (James Dunn, often her onscreen father, had possessed nice hands; devoid of the unsuspected hairs that perched spiderlike on some men's knuckles; the fingers tapered neatly and securely. They were not *grasping* like some hands she could name.)

Now we'll see what they've got in store for me, she thought resolutely, now that I'm—what am I? Hardly grown. But at least not a child anymore, that's for sure. And she thought with relish, no more *One-two, one-two, soft-shoe, without mistakes, or the box! The punishment box. Jack in the box.* Why, I'll ask him about the ship. I'll say, look here, this has gone on long enough, and something must be done! See if I won't!

When the duly assigned period of waiting had elapsed, she was beckoned to enter. The office, too, showcased evidence of a producer's many and various triumphs, films that had met with success, trinkets accumulated by a man with an eye to satisfying the curiosity of those summoned into his office, whose marveling glances he would survey while he felt with an obscure relish that he had arrived. There were movie awards, autographed photographs, an exquisite and pristine blotter.

She had a vision of what she ought to say, something hearty and chummy that would establish a clear basis between them. See here, she ought to say, old man, I'm all grown now, and I suppose you'll want to talk about the next picture, but I've got another subject to broach first. But somehow the words would not come; instead she merely stood there, looking at him. It was not in his face, exactly; it was not a trick of the light; it was as though the air between them had soured.

He arose from the desk, and with a jolt she observed that he was in his stockinged feet. (Was it stocking feet or stockinged feet? She was never entirely certain; there were cases to be made for both.) She had been warned of *this*.

But she had merely accepted the warning as a kind of friendly overture, a fact without relevance to herself, like the name of a long-extinct bird. Now she looked at him and thought, he is in his stockinged feet, I was *warned*, and a chill went through her. The fabric toe of his left sock was long and faintly dingy; it extended vacantly, obscenely, almost an inch beyond the foot.

Above the stockinged feet, his face rose unperturbed behind thin rimless glasses, suspended between a nose and ears that looked as though they had been fashioned from plasticine and then affixed. She felt with an obscure dread that he was going to say something, that he must say something, and that it would be something so dull and at once so dreadful that she would want to burst out laughing. Miss Temple, he would say, or Miss Curly-Top, or, the last time I saw you, weren't you still knee-high to a grasshopper. And she would have to laugh, and she clapped a hand over her mouth to prevent the mirth from escaping. His mouth opened. "Well, Miss Temple, I suppose you're just about all grown up, then." *It's a night trip. Into bed you'll hop.*

She had not yet gotten a good look at his hands. He was unfurling them, producing them, as a workman produces the implements of his trade, when the scent hit, emanating from the upper corner of the room, as though someone had squeezed it from the air. Another splash, a rope descending. Into what, into what?

"Lemonade," she said suddenly, and laughed. Her ship was coming in.

He looked baffled. On his back foot, she thought, and shivered, on his *stockinged back foot*. But of course he must smell it too; it was sharp, acid, and pungent, and it seemed to leak into the room from some crack in the masonry. Her nostrils were drowned with it.

"Miss Temple?" he asked, and there was an unmistakable *click*, metallic, from the underside of his desk.

Behind her the door slammed, locked, seemingly on its own, and she knew what the click had been. Ingenious! she thought. Such ingenuity to be brought to bear on something so pitiful and sordid. Then she thought, ingenious, not ingenuous. I wonder if that's something. That must be something.

Another splash. "Do you smell it?" she asked, lightly.

He shook his head. But how could he not? It was everywhere. The ship! The good ship!

"Come over here," he suggested. *And there you are. Happy landing on a chocolate bar.*

My god, she thought, is he actually going to, is he really going to try and *touch me*?

"I don't think I would like to," she heard herself saying; and anyway, she thought, so I was wrong, then, to think that I would ask him about the ship, and not the ship about him. A pity that it is docked only for such a short time; it would be too, too terrible to be pulled on board. (But where had it come from, anyway, that thought?)

He patted the edge of the desk invitingly, and the irrepressible surge of mirth went through her once again; does he believe me a cat? But the thought, no, not a cat, this is what you were *warned* about, there is no mistake. She was not certain whether to laugh or shriek with horror—so much the worse for him, not to be mistaken! All around them, unseen ropes were descending.

Now the air was thick with peppermint. *Good-good. Bonbon.* He began to make his way around the desk, steady creep of stockinged feet, and she began as steadily to retreat around the other side. He advanced and she retreated; he pursued and she inched rapidly back, and all the while in the air above them, it grew clearer and clearer, the outline of the ship; candy life preservers were thrown from it and caught up in steady outstretched hands, and the warbling voice of a dimpled familiar child with painfully curled vinegar-bright hair rose over all of it, *won't you be my crew.*

"I'm sorry," she whispered, and a mouth, moist, opened in the ceiling above him. *Mean old devil's food cake*, and there was a decided *squelch*, and she couldn't look anymore, crouched by the door and latticed her fingers over her eyes as the *squelch-crunch-slurp* began, and he vanished feet-first into its maw, mouth still frozen in a rictus of surprise.

She crouched there a long time waiting for the noises to cease. In the hallway, someone turned off the lights and walked all the way down, whistling to himself, tuneless. At last all was quiet and she dared to make her way across the floor again to where the socks lay vacant under the desk.

I'll say I ran around the desk, she thought, heart pounding, as she fumbled for the switch, not daring to open her eyes. The squelching noise persisted even though she knew, reasonably, there could be no cause; now the air was full of lemonade and brine. *Oooo weee. It's a night trip.* I'll say I ran around and around the desk and I don't know what happened next. And it may be that when they open the door, he will still be there, in his stock-inged feet, face unaltered, glasses not even mangled, nose still intact, eyes undigested, and there will be no sign of what has happened.

You'll awake with a tummy-ache.

She heard the door unlock itself and swing open, and she made her way nimbly and swiftly around the desk and stepped out into the hallway. The ship did not follow. My ship, she thought, approvingly. Good ship. Lollipop.

As she continued down the hall, she began to whistle. *It's a night trip*, she whistled. *It's a night trip.*

Witch Play Written in the 1950s as a Metaphor, by Arthur Miller

Arthur Miller had a lot to say about the Red Scare of the 1950s, which resulted in artists and writers being blacklisted for supposed Communist sympathies. And he said it all with his play The Crucible. *Whose original draft went something like this.*

Lights up on a New England town: Salem, in 1692, to be precise.

But is it really only in 1692 that people go on witch hunts to punish those who dare to think freely? Is it only in the parishes of the past, at the edge of forests as yet unhewn by the ax, that men are called upon to name names?

Enter Parris. Reverend Parris is the minister to this small community. His name is not Joseph McCarthy, but it might as well be. He is a sweaty man who loves to make lists, although he makes them with a quill pen rather than a ballpoint pen and a typewriter, and on his list are witches, not Communists, but is any sort of list, at any time, not fundamentally the cousin of all other such lists? He kneels and prays for more names to add to his list.

PARRIS: Where is Roy Cohn?*

Enter [Not Roy]. A word on Roy [it won't be Roy I'm just writing Roy in this draft]. Roy isn't a very evil, ambitious, grasping young lawyer, but he might as well be; he is some kind of Puritan man from the 1690s. But are not such men found in all communities, at all times?

NOT ROY COHN: Here I be.

PARRIS: Aye, I blink ye.†

NOT ROY: (confidentially, to Parris) Have ye hearkened the blab, neighbor Parris? Everyone in the community utters strongly of witches.

PARRIS: Aye, I blink ye.

Enter John Proctor. John Proctor is a man who if he lived in the present day would probably write plays, damn good ones, but some that weren't appreciated by audiences as much as they should have been, and if he were alive in the present day, Marilyn Monroe and he would have a fraught relationship that would ultimately end badly. He would be tall and virile in a quietly imposing way, so that when people saw him with Marilyn Monroe, they would say, mm,

---

* This isn't actually going to be the character's name I'm going to change it I just haven't yet

† The dialogue is intended to give the flavor of the past, but not actually bear any resemblance to the way people spoke in the past. I compromised by using words from the present, but ones that didn't make sense, so it kind of sounds like everyone's an old-timey sailor but also like someone went over normal dialogue very quickly with a thesaurus.

to themselves rather than, huh. This is a man who, if he
were, for example, called up before a committee, would die
before naming names. But I am getting ahead of myself.

PROCTOR: Good day to ye.

ROY COHN: Aye.

PARRIS: Nay. 'Tis a bad day, for much scurvy witchcraft be
noised about.

PROCTOR: (masculinely) Nay, there's not no such thing as
witchcraft.

ROY COHN: Communism does exist, however.[*]

PROCTOR: I tell ye there is not.

SEVERAL WOMEN WHO WERE THERE BUT I FORGOT
TO MENTION: (They say this line in a tone that conveys
how stunned they are by John Proctor's virility) If John
Proctor say nay, I think there be none.

OTHER WOMAN: John Proctor be the best man in all Salem.

PROCTOR: Nay.

John Proctor looks off solemnly as if he is concealing a
shameful secret in his breast. For John Proctor is not free
of personal, sexual shame: he has consorted out of wedlock
with a young, attractive woman, and he was very good at
it. But he feels bad, because of how he was raised.

---

[*] I'll fix this, but it'll be clear he's talking about communism.

Enter Abigail Williams. A word on Abigail. Abigail is very sexy and so forth, but now that she has gotten one taste of John Proctor, she is out of control! This era, like our own, is one where a woman's place is in the home and a man's place is mostly out of the house having an affair and then feeling bad about it and then testifying to a committee about how important it is to him to keep his own good name.

Enter Elizabeth Proctor. Elizabeth Proctor is John Proctor's wife, and she is also attractive but kind of judgy and standoffish, like a cat. She would be good at operating a vacuum cleaner but claiming that doing so made her too tired to have sex. Elizabeth says nothing, but she says it very loudly.

Exit Elizabeth Proctor, judgily. Not sure she needed to be in this scene, but I wanted to give the audience the context they needed to understand John Proctor's sex life. I will fix this though.

ABIGAIL: John, I long for ye. Speak me but one soft word, John, or if ye say me nay, I shall blab to Roy Cohn that your wife be a communist. Be my stallion, John.

JOHN PROCTOR: (ambiguously) Nay!

ABIGAIL: Nay, John Proctor? Or neigh?

JOHN PROCTOR: Nay.

ABIGAIL: I saw Goody Proctor with Elia Kazan! I saw Goody Proctor with Lillian Hellman! And all three of them were with the Devil, who is communism!

ROY COHN: Do you have any other names, Abigail?

PARRIS: Aye, name us some names. We be compiling a list.

ABIGAIL: I don't, but John Proctor does.

JOHN PROCTOR: (unnerved) Nay.

ELIZABETH PROCTOR: John!*

JOHN PROCTOR: I shall not stand for this! This feels like some sort of a—a hunt of some kind, that thing whereof many innocent people be needlessly condemned, on no evidence. Like—out-of-control McCarthyism!

ABIGAIL: Bring in Giles Corey!

GILES COREY: (being crushed under a rock) I'm local farmer Giles Corey, and I'm here to have rocks put on my chest and confess whether or not I'm a witch—and it looks like you've still got plenty of rocks.

The rock is an ordinary rock, to drive home the fact that this might happen now. Although today it might not be a rock at all, but a list, or series of lists.

GILES COREY: (dying, crushed by a rock) I underestimated how many rocks you had when I said I was going to have rocks put on my chest first and confess afterward.

ROCK: I regret killing Giles Corey, but I am glad that because he neither confessed nor denied being a witch, his family got to keep his farm.

---

* I guess she is back in the scene now. I will fix all of this.

ROY COHN: So, John Proctor. See what happened to Giles
   Corey. How will you testify?

JOHN PROCTOR: My good name is very important to me. I
   will not name the names of others. Myself, sure, but others,
   no. I only have one good name: John Proctor. Others have
   called it an okay name at best, but to me, it's a good name.
   And I won't sully it . . . not for the world!*

ELIZABETH: This is the most attracted I have ever been to you,
   John.

---

* This is a very good speech to give if you're ever invited to testify to a committee, and I intend to use a version of it myself when I have to go testify to
the House Un-American Activities Committee, which I have to do right
now, but then I'll come right back and edit this draft.

What If They Censored Books, and It Was Bad, by Ray Bradbury

It was a pleasure to burn. Millay on Mondays, Whitman on Wednesdays, Faulkner on Fridays! Guy Montag had never read a single book, but he knew all the names of the writers whose books it was his job to burn. His face was scorched from all the burning. He lived in a dystopia.

"This is your job?" asked Clarisse McClellan, who was almost seventeen and existed to awaken Guy Montag from his torpor using whimsy and precocity. "This is your full-time job?"

"Yes," Guy Montag said, a little uncertainly. "I am a fireman, and in this society of ours, firemen *burn* books instead of stopping fires, which I hear that they once used to do."

"And people pay you money to do this?" Clarisse said, as whimsically and effervescently as Guy Montag's wife wouldn't have.

"Yes, because all the houses are completely fireproof now," Guy said patiently. "Because we fixed it, with technology."

"I'm going to accept that what you said about fireproofing is true," Clarisse said, "although it made limited sense, because I am still hung up on the fireman thing. You are paid an annual salary and benefits for going to houses to burn books? Just books? Not things in general. Just to burn books, exclusively?"

"Yes, like my father and grandfather before me."

"Wouldn't all the books have been gotten rid of by now?"

Clarisse asked. "I mean, Jesus, where are all these books coming from?"

"I don't know," Guy said. "I never thought about it."

"And everyone's still literate?"

"I think so," Guy said. "Yes. Earlier my wife was reading a TV script that she got in the mail, and that was encouraged, actually."

"So what makes a book dangerous?"

"I think it's the ideas inside it that are dangerous," Guy said. "It's, like, a metaphor. Society has turned on readers and intellectuals, and now every wall is a television, and we put seashell radios in our ears, and we are all deeply unhappy, and instead of a speed limit we have a speed *minimum*."

"I'm sorry," Clarisse said, "I understand all that. But if people are allowed and encouraged to read scripts, why can't they just print out a book on individual sheets of paper and read it that way? Wouldn't that solve the problem and keep them out of trouble with the authorities?"

"You ask too many questions," Guy said.

"Is it that people like the old book smell? It's a great smell, of course. But if it's the difference between having someone paid by the state come to your home to destroy your belongings with fire—are you paid by the state, by the way, or is it a private enterprise?"

Some nuclear warplanes flew overhead very loudly at that exact moment so that Guy did not have to answer this question.

"Don't get me wrong," Clarisse was saying, when the noise had abated, "it's a powerful metaphor. Really makes you think. But the fact that it's just having a print book in your home that will make you run afoul of the authorities seems like a ridiculous loophole to me. Wouldn't people just constantly plant them in the homes of people they disliked? Especially if books are so readily available that after three generations there are still enough of them around for this to be your full-time job. Also, if there are still enough of them around now that this is your full-time job, hasn't it occurred to anyone that this system is not working? And what about technical manuals? If you really need a large technical manual in your home, do you have to print it out on individual loose sheets of paper so that the firemen won't come? What about telephone directories?"

"Clarisse," Montag said, "you ask too many questions."

"I mean," Clarisse said, "it's just, it seems—I'm sorry—incredibly inefficient. If there are still enough books that you have a job, then maybe instead of firemen, they should have Guys Who Smash Printing Presses and Tackle This Problem on the Supply End. Maybe they should pass a law against bookbinding. It seems like really what they are afraid of is bindings, not books."

"We go to houses with fire because of the terrifying power of the written word," Montag said. "To show people that censorship is bad."

"It seems pretty heavy-handed," Clarisse said. She plucked a dandelion and savored it, which Guy Montag had never seen anyone do even once because he lived in a dystopia, and nobody in it was allowed to savor anything.

"Don't question society," Guy Montag said.

"Sorry, Guy," Clarisse said, "I'm not like other girls, and I question society sometimes." She laughed. She had a beautiful face like the moon. Montag had never looked at the moon because, again, this was a dystopia.

"I—" Montag started, but then fortunately more planes went overhead, destroying the entire city, and he did not have to answer.

1950s Recipes

Ham Salad

Weird Egg

Gelatinous Mass (Circular)

Other Noun You Wouldn't Expect to Be Followed
by Salad, Followed by Salad

Wiener Porcupine

Dill Pickle Panopticon

The Hideous Eye on All the Currency

Apple Full of Razors and Mercury

Casserole You Don't Remember Making But It Must
Have Gotten into the House Somehow

Bouillon Slaw

Soft Cheese Replica of Moon

Cheese with a Flag in It

Gray Dip

Green Dip

Red Dip

Entertainment Cracker

Sherbet

Gelatinous Mass (Hexagonal)

Hot Off-White Thing in Bowl

Salty Sticks

Dry Lattice Cracker

Wadded-Up Cocktail Napkin You Put in Your Mouth by Mistake Because It Was on the Tray

Salami with Cream Cheese and Salt Stacked Together into a Little Pizza

Aspic

Little Tube of Mercury for Fun

Big Glass of Alcohol

A Pineapple by Itself

The Sound of Masculine Laughter, a Whiff of Cigarette Smoke

Tomato Pie

Brylcreem

Ham Salad

SERVES: 16
PREP TIME: You won't have time to attend college or pursue any goals outside the home.
INGREDIENTS: One ham, cubed

INSTRUCTIONS: Cube ham. Add one jar Hellmann's mayonnaise and sour cream to taste. Serve in ceramic tray shaped like a fish. Delicious!

Weird Egg

SERVES: 16
PREP TIME: The best years of your life.
INGREDIENTS: One dozen eggs. Some celery. Mayonnaise.
INSTRUCTIONS: Boil an egg. Take what was inside it out and then put all the mayonnaise you have into it and put it back in. The egg was not complete until it was given its mayonnaise. It is complete now!

Big Glass of Alcohol

SERVES: One
INSTRUCTIONS: Take an entire container of gin and just pour it into a big glass! Take it to your business lunch. If serving at home, be sure to put the glass near a jar of mayonnaise so it feels at home.

Hot Off-White Thing in Bowl

SERVES: 16
INGREDIENTS: 3 cans of Cream of Chicken Soup
3 cans of Cream of Mushroom Soup
Sour cream
INSTRUCTIONS: Put all these ingredients together in a big bowl and simmer them! This is either a dip or a main course or a dessert, no one is sure!

Aspic

SERVES: 8
INGREDIENTS: Tomato paste. Resentment.
INSTRUCTIONS: It is both always ready and never not congealed enough. Don't serve. Keep it in your fridge for years.

Tomato Pie

SERVES: 9
INGREDIENTS: Store-bought pie shell
Canned tomatoes
Canned cheese
INSTRUCTIONS: Put canned things into store-bought thing. Bake for some amount of time. Leave on window ledge to cool, and then serve at a party or slip it into the mailbox of your worst enemy.

Other McCarthy Lists

I have here in my hand a list of 205 . . . a list of names
that were made known to the Secretary of State as
being members of the Communist Party.

—*Senator Joseph McCarthy*

I have here in my hand a list of 205 . . .

+ pushups I've done
+ separate distinct occasions my mother has said she
  loved me
+ things I like about myself, I could easily list all of them
  right here
+ swell ideas I've had that would make fine sitcoms if
  Hollywood were not overrun with commies and who
  knows what all
+ men, serious respected men, who think I'm a good fellow, who say nice things about me when I'm absent
+ close intimate personal friends who would help me
  move
+ people who would definitely come to my funeral and
  for the right reasons
+ women who have all agreed to sleep with me because
  of what they describe, their words not mine, as my raw
  sexual charisma

+ different types of raisin
+ women willing to tell the Secretary of State that I am a dynamite lay in addition to those first 205 women
+ people who say nice things about me behind my back
+ dentists willing to defer to my judgment
+ groceries
+ communists (female) who have agreed to sleep with me

Two Pages of *Catcher in the Rye* That Were Removed Before Publication But Maybe Shouldn't Have Been

John Hinckley Jr. and Mark David Chapman both blamed Catcher in the Rye *for their decisions to shoot Ronald Reagan and John Lennon, respectively.*

"By the way," I said to Phoebe. We were walking through Central Park. I don't even know what the hell I said it for. Sometimes a thing just comes out of your mouth. "I don't think anybody ought to shoot the president." Phoebe kept looking at me. "Or John Lennon," I said.

"John Lennon?"

"I don't see why anybody would want to shoot them," I said, "either the president or John Lennon, but I don't think he ought to do it, that's all."

"I don't see why anybody would want to either," Phoebe said.

I never knew what the hell to say to her, so I kept going. I was flogging the subject pretty well into the ground. "Do you ever have thoughts like that?" I said.

"Like wanting to shoot the president?" Phoebe asked.

"Like wanting people to know," I said, "that if they want to shoot the goddamn president or John Lennon, they'd better think twice about it, is all."

"Not particularly," she said.

"Well, I do," I said. "Have thoughts like that, I mean. You know what I would really like to be?"

"No," old Phoebe said.

"You know that song, if a body catch a body coming through the rye? I keep picturing all these kids, all these little kids, playing some game in this big field of rye and all. Thousands of kids, and nobody's around, nobody big, I mean, except for me. And I'm standing on the edge of some crazy cliff. And what I have to do is go up to those kids, one by one, and say, I know you're feeling alienated as all hell from society, or something, but the one thing you can't do is go and shoot the president of the goddamn United States."

"Or John Lennon," Phoebe said.

"I wouldn't want you to do that," I said. "That's what I would say, to those kids, I mean."

Phoebe nodded solemnly.

"Who the hell knows why somebody wants to go and shoot the president," I said, "or John Lennon. But I would think about that, and I would tell them, I don't know what you want to go and do a thing like that for, but if you think you're going to impress the actress Jodie Foster by doing it, you'd better think a second goddamn time. Only a phony would do something that goddamn stupid, and Jodie Foster won't be impressed one bit. That's what I'd say," I said, "to those kids in the rye. And they would call me the Guy in the Rye Who Tells You You'd Better Not Shoot John Lennon or the President Even If You Want to Impress Jodie Foster. That's all I'd really like to be, the Guy in the Rye Who Tells You You'd Better Not Shoot John Lennon or the President Even If You Want to Impress Jodie Foster, Because It's Not Going to Impress Her, and all."

Phoebe tilted her head to the side.

"Now," I said, "let's go feed the goddamn ducks."

Giovanni's Escape Room

I'm sad that this crossover venture didn't get off the ground after the initial marketing pamphlet, but here is that pamphlet.

Presenting... GIOVANNI'S ESCAPE ROOM! The only Escape Room inspired by the James Baldwin classic! Can you ever escape Giovanni's room and be happy with your fiancée, Hella? Will you ever be honest with yourself? Or will you "press, in great pain, through a maze of false signals and abruptly locking doors"?

The puzzles:

+ Come to Europe as an American and leave it happy.
+ Using only a 10,000-franc note, locate the striking young Italian bartender who will be the love of your life.
+ Successfully answer Giovanni's questions about time and America in order to get yourself invited to his room. (Hint: Don't play it safe, or you will wind up alone, trapped in your own dirty body forever!)
+ You, Jacques, Guillaume, and Giovanni must all leave Guillaume's bar together in a taxi. Who should sit where? What if Giovanni takes your hand? What will you do then?

- In his excitement Giovanni has torn up all his severance pay from Guillaume's bar. Help him tape it back together so that you can afford food!
- Hidden somewhere in the detritus of Giovanni's room (which is not the garbage of Paris itself; Giovanni's metaphor was inapt), there is Giovanni's own regurgitated life. Help Giovanni find it! It should be somewhere beneath the violin music and the unplayed violin, or maybe under the rotten, wrinkly potato.
- Help Giovanni knock out some of the bricks in the wall of his room to make room for a bookcase. It's possible that doing so can create the room you need to be happy here!
- Memorize Giovanni's face.
- Avoid slipping on anguish and fear and losing your balance, dignity, and pride.
- Successfully explain, aloud, to even a single person your emotional state at any time.
- Everyone has his Eden, the home he always leaves, which will always remain home so long as he does not endeavor to return. Locate yours. Hint: it is in this room!
- Write a letter to your father back in America about needing money without mentioning Giovanni or otherwise arousing his suspicions.

You have five months, those delicate months from the start of spring until the middle of summer!

50 States of Grey

He glanced at the mangled form before him. It was still not perfect. It had been pressed and squeezed, but not enough. Though horribly distended in parts, and horribly condensed in others, it still lacked the form that had so thrilled his imagination. Though pale, it was not sufficiently so. Though so narrow at some points as to confuse anyone who gazed upon it, it was not yet perfect. Another tiny modification, 1 percent shaved off here, another 1 percent added there, and it would begin to take the form that he had long dreamed, the one that would answer his wish, that would embody fully his vision.

"No," he said. "We have to keep gerrymandering."

KLAXON!

+ You've just received a letter from your fiancée, Hella! She'll be in Paris in nine days! You're up against the clock now. You'd better get out of Giovanni's room!
+ Pick up your suitcase. Stand with your hand on the door. Giovanni is in bed with a glass of cognac in his hand, looking gray and pale in the morning light. Walk through the door away from him and from his

body *without* begging him to forgive you or giving his
body permanent sway over yourself. (This one's tricky!)

✦ Tell Hella that you want to escape Giovanni's room
and you want to get out of Paris. So do it! You said you
wanted to do it. Or is it that what you are really trying
to escape is yourself?

✦ Successfully burn out, through contact with your fiancée Hella, the reality of Giovanni and the memory of
his touch.

SIREN!

✦ Uh-oh! You must not have done that right. Your
abrupt departure destroyed something in Giovanni
and he has done a murder. You have exactly ten days
to hold it together for your fiancée as Giovanni's exe-
cution approaches. All you have to do is not confess to
her that you love him or pick up any sailors.

✦ Either remember your Eden or forget it forever. Both
require a different kind of strength.

It's already those delicate months from the start of spring until
the middle of summer! You'd better hurry!

Allen Ginsberg's *Howl* (Original Dog Draft)

Nobody knows this, but actually Allen Ginsberg's famous poem
Howl *was dictated to him by a dog he befriended one afternoon
in San Francisco. That is why it is called* Howl. *The dog was fine
with him adapting it, though, because he was a dog and wanted
what was best for Allen.*

Here is the dog draft.

i.

I have seen the best canines of my generation destroyed by
　　madness, barking hysterical sweatered
Dragging themselves to the unfrequented rainy parks at dawn
　　barking for an easy stick
Angel-minded mutts who went off-leash not on purpose,
　　yearning for the wild, for that old natural something
Who bark and dog treat and lolling-tongue and eyed came
　　sniffing at the tail-ends of strangers at the tail-ends of
　　strange evenings
Who lifted dainty legs and wrote their names on fire-hydrants
　　in grand symbolic gestures, and barked with pride and
　　satisfaction
Who foamed at the mouth with delight of greeting, turning
　　around thrice and again thrice

Who ball-chased in the mornings and the evenings in the wet
grass of public parks, barking with delight

Who watched tennis ball after tennis ball vanish into the
unknown of Bush and Thicket and were bewildered

Who yearned for absent human staring at the sad vastness of
Door

Who devoured shoes and shoelaces and were chastened by finger-
pointing and uttering of the unholy shibboleth "Bad Dog"

Who devoured nothing and chewed placidly on Bone and
were nevertheless rebuked because their concomitant
felines had done something to a fern and upchucked on
suggestively proximate rugs

Who barked for reasons and barked for no reasons at all and
whined a high whine sometimes, train-lonesome, and were
met with replies or not met with replies

Who made unrequited love with the panty-hosed legs of
strangers and the pants legs of strangers and angel dogs
with whom they were not acquainted and devil dogs with
whom they were acquainted

Who stared at a wall or a spot on a wall sometimes for no
reason and barked with alarm

Who jumped as though by instinct on the one person
who said she disliked dogs and licked and barked with
satisfaction of disproof

Who preened in content at greeting of old man on street
corner and showed hint of Belly

Who were once puppies with joyous abundance of limb and
superfluity of paw

Who forgot at times that they were not puppies still, and
overturned tables forgetting

Who went out on trips in myriad night-cars, panting through

window, while JK, secret hero of these poems, gave them
neck scritches and belly rubs

Who leaped upon Sofa and were greeted with loud slaps of
rolled up newspaper and returned to carpet level, still
reeling with ecstatic visions

Who walked all afternoon and got tangled up in Leash
and brought triumphant home as an oblation a thrilling
Sidewalk Object of unclear provenance to consternation
and yell of all human observers

Who bit strangers on the ankle and were not sorry

Who pursued squirrels and were pursued by squirrels

Who barked at mailmen and were not pursued

Who frequented dog parks to fraternize with others of their
kind

Who fretted at long absence and were on verge of eating
forbidden chocolate when doorbell rang with news of Return

Who went tearing around the house wild with doorbell and
excited

Who received justified praise for sitting and unjustified praise
for not sitting

Who leaped eagerly into cars to go for rides and woke up
dazed in the cold light of Vet

Who transported upon steel tables had their balls transported
to regions unknown and returned home chastened in Cone

Who overturned only one symbolic ping-pong table and not
even in protest just because they were startled and panicked
at a noise

Who barked all night in agonies of terror at Bug

Who had their bellies scratched by angels on street corners
and wagged with delight

Who received treats from those human seraphim, the humans

Who stayed and shook hands like associates in business and
counterfeited the whole human condition before lying
down on rug to nap a hundred years.

ii.

What malign being extruded the filling from the couch
cushions and ate the chicken that was left out a moment
upon the counter? Bad dog!
Filth! Disorder! Trash cans overturned! Puddle on hardwood!
Bad! Down! Off! Bad dog!
Bad dog who uproots the houseplants! Bad dog who shreds
the sofa cushions! Bad dog who steals chocolate! Bad dog
who humps carpet! Bad dog who jumps in greeting when
jumping is expressly forbidden!
Bad dog whose eyes breathe thunder! Bad dog who barks at rain-
clouds! Bad dog whose encounters at dog park are merciless!
Bad dog who eats my luncheon! Bad dog whose reek is
skunky! Bad dog who growled at Grandma! Bad dog whose
turd is on carpet! Bad dog who shakes off rain in doorway!
Bad dog who growls at package! Bad dog whose name is
unheeded! Bad dog whose blood runs with purloined bacon!
Bad dog who is on sofa! Bad dog who remains on sofa!
Bad dog in corner who sits lonely! Bad dog who rides in
car sadly! Bad dog who curls up in crate! Bad dog who is
nevertheless Dog! Come here you.

iii.

Human! I'm with you on sofa
Where you're muddier than I am

I'm with you on sofa

Where you growl at the TV

I'm with you on sofa

Where your pocket is treatless and your eyes water

I'm with you on sofa

Where you whine and growl into the telephone

I'm with you on sofa

Where television is displaying its enormous bounty

I'm with you on sofa

Where you and I possess an unspoken understanding

I'm with you on sofa

When the phone sings rejection and the pizza arrives

I'm with you on sofa

Where America barks all night and won't let us sleep

I'm with you on sofa

Where the game is on and your lousy team is losing

I'm with you on sofa

Where cat is eying us mistrustfully

I'm with you on sofa

When my muzzle is graying with time

I'm with you on sofa

When there is no point in telling me to get down off of sofa

I'm with you on sofa

Where you scratch my head and murmur encouragements

I'm with you on sofa

Where we snore noisily together

In my dreams the door opens upon bounteous wilderness
     of squirrels, and I hear your voice beckoning Good Dog,
     Good Dog, let's go take a walk.

The Night They Came Up with All the Currency

Here is a completely correct transcript of the session at the U.S. Mint when they designed all the currency.

The Penny: First off is the penny, which has the side of Abraham Lincoln's head (NO HAT!) on the front and the Lincoln Memorial on the back. We argued about the hat. Trevor said if we did it to scale, the top of the hat would stick off the side and make the penny sharp and unpleasant to carry around, and most people agreed he was probably right. It is worth one cent, which is another way of saying it is worth one penny. We were thinking sort of an orange coppery color for this one, so we are making it out of a small amount of copper, which means that it technically costs more than one cent to produce, but I think that is fine because the aesthetic is so strong. We are calling it the penny because that is what they call something similar in England.

Nickel: Next comes the nickel, which is worth five pennies (cents). It is a little bigger than the penny because it's worth more! It has Thomas Jefferson (also a side view) on the front and—no, not the Jefferson Memorial, Thomas Jefferson's actual house on the back. We absolutely, definitely remembered there was a Jefferson Memorial; we just thought his house was cooler. Plus we don't want people who learn about this country only from the currency to think that we're like, super into Thomas Jefferson, so we thought if we just had his face and his house instead of also a picture of a shrine we built for him, it would be a little more neutral? The observer will be like, "Well, they definitely like Thomas Jefferson, but they're not weird about it." Then again, his house was a plantation so maybe this is just as bad? We are calling this one the nickel because that is the material that 25 percent of it is made out of. It is mostly made of copper but we are not calling it that. (Trevor said this naming was weird and inconsistent, but we just want to celebrate metals!)

Dime: Okay, we have another coin for you and you're going to love it! It's got Franklin Delano Roosevelt's head on the front, and on the back we've got some plants and a torch! I think it speaks for itself. Also we don't want people to know where Franklin Delano Roosevelt lived. The torch is a symbol. We're calling it the dime because we think that's Latin for something. It's either tenth or day; we printed it on all the dimes already so please don't tell us if we're wrong. It's not bigger than the nickel or the penny because it's worth the most of all of them. This is to show people not to judge things by appearances! It is also silver-colored and made of copper and nickel but we aren't going to allude to that in its name.

Quarter: I bet you were wondering how we would top the dime, and the answer is: with the quarter! The quarter is worth one quarter of a dollar, so it's called a quarter. This makes a lot of sense, and we wish we'd come up with it earlier when we were deciding what to call the nickel, but I guess it's too late. This one will be really big because it's worth a lot, just to keep people on their toes about judging by appearances. It is also mostly copper.

It will have George Washington on the front, and on the back it will have a big bird. I love all you guys, and we're doing so well at this. Isn't it great how all the pictures are different?

Dollar: This one is going to be a piece of paper!!!! It is called a dollar because it is worth one dollar, a word we made up, which the Oxford dictionaries say comes "from early Flemish or Low German *daler*, from German *T(h)aler*, short for *Joachimsthaler*, a coin from the silver mine of Joachimsthal ('Joachim's Valley')." It's important to remind people about the good times we all had in Joachim's Valley. It's going to have George Washington on the front, but this time he'll be facing us, which is basically like having a whole new person on it. On the back we want a creepy lidless eye hovering over a pyramid. This sends a strong message to people who felt like they understood what the currency was doing. This will be fun for people who want to go to other countries and show them pieces of our currency with the houses and birds and things on the back, and then say, "I bet you cannot guess what is on the back of this!" and this will allow them to win money when abroad, which will help to strengthen the Joachim's Valley Currency Unit. How will we keep people from just printing out their own versions of this and using it as money? Do not be silly; nobody owns a printer anymore. Also the paper this is printed on will be, like, weird paper, and it will be kind of greenish.

Two Dollar Bill: This is a weird increment, but we're going to make it be LEGAL TENDER BABY! It's worth two dollars, but it's a whole different piece of paper with an entirely different design. I cannot think of anything this would be more convenient for, but some things are more important than being convenient. On the front will be Thomas Jefferson again because I guess we're actually kind of obsessed with him, and on the back will be a picture of a picture of some people standing in a room signing the Constitution. Trevor said we shouldn't put people on both sides, but we were drunk with power so we did. Plus this is basically a secret bonus bill, and it's not like anyone will ever see or use it. We're still sticking with the greenish theme though.

Five Dollar Bill: This will have Abe Lincoln but facing forward on the front, and on the back the Lincoln Memorial. This is definitely the most normcore bill yet.

Ten Dollar Bill: Alexander Hamilton on the front, but like a sexy picture of him, and on the back we'll have a picture of the building where he worked. Not when he was actually working there, but the building inspired by the concept of what his job was. The U.S. Treasury Building. Come to think of it, this isn't a universally famous, beloved building, so we should probably label it so people know what it is. He's not a president and everyone else has been president, but that's fine. It's good that we don't have to just pick presidents, because some of them were pretty lousy human beings, and it would be bad to have to carry their pictures around all the time.

Twenty Dollar Bill: After having just established that we could put anyone on the bill, we have decided to pick Andrew Jackson for this one! In our defense, we are not doing so great at this anymore. This is going to have Andrew Jackson on the front, and on the back I guess the building where he worked? The White House, that is, not any other building he might have worked in during his long career. Now that we know we can have an unrelated group picture or painting on the back, maybe we should put something to draw people's focus away from the man responsible for the Indian Removal Act and for, you know, trying to help Aaron Burr invade Mexico and make himself its king. Actually, can we get him off it and put Harriet Tubman on?

Fifty Dollar Bill: Okay, moving on, this one has Ulysses S. Grant on the front, and I guess a building on the back, but not a building that Ulysses S. Grant spent any time in or liked! The Capitol! Why not, right? It's a nice building. Better than the weird eye pyramid.

One Hundred Dollar Bill: Benjamin Franklin will be on the front of this, because we once again remembered that it can be anyone! But not just any Ben Franklin: Ben Franklin with a hideous blue stripe! Nobody wanted this; we just messed up. On the back will be Independence Hall, a building from Philadelphia, because that was Benjamin Franklin's favorite place, a place he really connected with, and we heard the Grant complaints.

Five Hundred Dollar Bill: Now we are just going crazy! This bill will have William McKinley on it OR John Marshall OR General Sherman OR Charles Sumner or a random painting of Civilization, just, like, the concept! Nobody is going to use this bill, we hope! No idea what is on the back. Honestly feel free to counterfeit this one; it's more of a template!

One Thousand Dollar Bill: At the beginning of this process, we all said, "Dewitt Clinton should be on the money" and even though Trevor said no, we held on to the idea. The only other idea we came up with was Grover Cleveland, which is fine because if you see a guy with a mustache on the currency, you probably assume it's Teddy Roosevelt or William Howard Taft, whom we feel bad we forgot, so this kills a lot of birds with a single stone. We also thought it would be really funny to put Alexander Hamilton on this one again so it looks like somebody made a typo on a ten dollar bill and now it's worth one hundred times as much money. This is fun! Nobody will use these!

Five Thousand Dollar Bill: James Madison. Why not!

Ten Thousand Dollar Bill: This one is going to have Supreme Court justice SALMON P. CHASE on the front, and we're putting the Pilgrims on the back. This will help to cut down on bank robberies because if anyone sees this bill with Salmon P. Chase on the front and the pilgrims on the back that claims to be worth $10,000, they will be like, there is no way in hell this is real money, and they will stop robbing the bank and go home. Which is more likely: that there was a Supreme Court justice named Salmon P. Chase (a fish name, not a people name) and nobody has heard of him but also we thought he was so important that we put this unrecognizable man on the piece of money that is worth the most of any piece of currency, or that this . . . did not happen? Who would look at this and say, confidently, "This is for sure real money"? This bill also sets up lots of other fun scenarios, like, someone brings you home a salmon bill and you say, "Are you sure that is real? That's not how Salmon P. Chase looked!" and who is going to be like, "No, I'm confident that this is a good picture of Salmon P. Chase! I would know that face anywhere!" Anyway none of this is real, we hope!

The Sun-Maid Correspondence

Lorraine Hansberry was the Pulitzer Prize–winning author of the play A Raisin in the Sun. *She also received mail.*

Dear Ms. Hansberry,

We here at Sun-Maid, A Raisin Company (They're Our Raisin D'Etre) are so thrilled and wish to congratulate you upon the success of *A Raisin in the Sun.* As a gesture of our appreciation, we would like to send you a large basket of complimentary raisins from California's number-one raisin-producing farmer association. Is this a good address to send them? We are so thrilled that the highest form of grape has served to inspire one as gifted as yourself. We have long felt that the raisin deserved a moment in, as you so aptly put it, the sun (our raisins are all sun-ripened, so we know the process well!), and we could not be more delighted by your choice of subject and its Broadway success.

As we like to say, raisins are not just for the kitchen anymore. You know the sensation that you have upon biting into a cookie and discovering that there are raisins in it? Now multiply that feeling across all forms of expression! Imagine America's delight at finding unexpected raisins not only in their cookies or breakfast cereals but also in their novels, their plays, their musicals, their short films, their newsreels! You name it, the raisin will elevate it! I cannot tell you what a relief it is to discover someone else who shares this conviction. I had begun to think I was entirely alone. I have been writing to Tennessee Williams for years begging him to put raisins in his plays, but all my letters come back unopened. And then, like a bolt out of the blue, you came, and—you knew, intuitively, that what Broadway needed was the very thing that I had always advocated. Bless you. You have the wisdom and understanding of a god, and the raisin is fortunate to have you as an acolyte.

We would love to partner with you to offer some sort of intermission snack bag. Do let us know to whom we can address that request! Anything that puts raisins in front of the American public is bound to meet with success.

Keep raisin hell, Ms. Hansberry, you're doing grape,

Sun-Maid (Kevin)

Dear Kevin,

I would be happy to accept the basket of raisins, but I don't think there is any point in affiliating them with the play. As surely someone there must know, even if you don't, the title is an allusion to a poem by Langston Hughes, in which raisins are used as a simile for a what happens to a dream deferred. There aren't any raisins in the play.

Sincerely,
Lorraine Hansberry

Ms. Hansberry,

I am still reeling from the impact of your last letter. The words still swim before my eyes. They crowd thickly at the edge of my vision like a clump of raisins that have gotten stuck together at the bottom of a box; I am haunted and undone by them. No!

Raisins! In the Play! Surely you jest, Ms. Hansberry. But you must not jest about so vital a matter. Such betrayal, such rejection!, is unfathomable to me. Not since Tennessee Williams's long silence have I been so let down by anyone or anything.

No raisins in *A Raisin in the Sun!* Next you will tell me that there is no Godot in *Waiting for Godot*, that there is no seagull in *The Seagull*, that Hamlet features no ham whatsoever. No raisins in *Raisin*? I suppose there are no cars in *Carmen*, then, and I am not going to find anything in *Moby-Dick* that the title promises at all! Next you will have me believe that there is no Iceman in *The Iceman Cometh*, that there is no cat in *Cat on a Hot Tin Roof*, that all of Broadway sits enthroned upon a dais of hypocrisy, wrapped in a tissue of lies! I suppose you are going to tell me that *not a single play's title accurately describes what is going to be contained in it!* I suppose there is no customization to be found in *As You Like It*! I suppose in *Show Boat* we are just told about the boat and not shown it at all! I bet there's no Harvey in *Harvey*, no crucible in *The Crucible*, and if there were ever a play called *Fun Home*, I bet that home would not even be remotely fun! Is there even a hat in *Fedora?* Does the Salesman even die?

Your callous indifference to raisins except as metaphor does something to me that a raisin has never done: it disappoints. I can't take back the raisins, which are already on their way to you, but I wish that I could. You are no true apostle of this glorious fruit. All my dreams have shriveled.

Kevin

P.S. I was going to share the delightful information that you and the woman in our iconic logo share a name (Lorraine), but now I won't.

Dear Kevin,

I'm afraid you are right about the shows you mentioned. I'm sorry you got the news from me. But thank you for the raisins. They were delicious. I used some of them for a pie.

Sincerely,
Lorraine Hansberry

Dear Ms. Hansberry,

I am so sorry about the letter you just received. Kevin is very eager to put raisins in front of the American public, and I think he may have gotten a bit carried away. You observed that he was clearly not familiar with your work, and that the raisin was an allusion to the writing of Langston Hughes. Do you have Langston's address? We would love to send him some raisins.

Sincerely,
Sun-Maid (Theo)

Ayn Rand's
The Little Engine That Could But Preferred Not To

Ayn "That's Not Writing, That's Typing"* Rand didn't believe that people should have nice things because of something called Objectivism that she made up.

(NB: This is not a book for children. It is permissible to read this book aloud in a room where a child happens to be, but only if the reader is genuinely interested in the book for his own sake, not from some mistaken, altruistic notion of benefiting the child, which will undermine the whole function and message of the book. If a man in a room is reading the book aloud for his own satisfaction and a child happens to enter the room, he need not stop; neither, however, should he feel obliged to continue. He owes nothing to the child. Yes, a child will benefit from this book. Anyone who reads this book will derive benefit from it, for it embraces objectivism, the one true philosophy that all books should embrace but do not, due to pink influences in publishing houses and the weak, misguided empathy of most authors who do not believe that "man's own happiness" is the "moral purpose

---

* Actually, Truman Capote said this about Jack Kerouac, but it also accurately describes my feelings about Ayn Rand.

of his life, with productive achievement as his noblest activity, and reason as his only absolute." As such, this book stands alone; whether it is appreciated is a reflection not of the book's worth but of the reader's worth.)

Chug. Chug. Chug. (Author's note: This onomatopoeia [though certainly preferable to the asinine "choo choo"] is at best a flimsy imitation of the majestic sound of a locomotive, and one reading this book aloud or, preferably, an industrious child reading the book to herself so as not to be a parasite upon her parents' time and resources must endeavor to reproduce more faithfully the noise of a train, which cannot be conveyed adequately in print.)

The little train went along the track. It is good for a train to be about its business. Men and trains ought always to be about their business, pursuing their own particular excellence.

The track was in disrepair (a consequence of the railroad management's passivity).

The train carried toys to redistribute to children. (A disgraceful errand!)

The train was chugging up a hill when it came suddenly to a halt. Something was not right with the train. (In addition to the self-inflicted spiritual rot caused by the train's altruism, something was mechanically wrong with it.)

The toys aboard the train were, of course, parasites. They could offer it no useful assistance.

The train was forced to wait (passively) on its stretch of track for an engine to come along. It is always thus with those who have nothing of value to offer and throw themselves upon the mercy of others.

Along came a Shiny New Engine. It was a powerful, impressive machine that I for one would like to see go into a tunnel. (Edifying and doubtless a pleasant experience for the tunnel.) "Help us," the dolls and toys called to the Shiny New Engine.

"No!" the Shiny New Engine uttered, courageously. "I owe nothing to you! I will not help you! Help yourselves!"

"We are meant to be given to children to play with," said the toys and dolls.

"Your request is immoral and vicious," said the Shiny New Engine. "A train's first duty is to itself. I am a passenger train, and I am concerned with my work."

The mighty passenger train chugged past in a triumphant blaze. I quiver violently when I think of that majestic train doing its duty. (It is not inappropriate to mention this; any child reading this work will grow up someday and understand the feelings provoked by trains, especially large, shiny trains who understand the principles of objectivism.)

Next came another train, a Big Strong Engine, and again the dolls cried out to it for assistance. (Anyone reading this volume aloud should do his best to make the voice he attributes to the parasitic dolls and toys one that inspires absolute, instantaneous, utter loathing. The voice of a sheep, or something even lower than a sheep.)

"I will not help you," said the Big Strong Engine. "You have no claim on me. If you were logs of strong, serviceable wood instead of frivolous knickknacks, it would be a different story. To haul logs is my work, and I am concerned with my work."

"Then how are we to get up the mountain and give these toys to the children?" the dolls and toys cried.

The Big Strong Engine shrugged. "I am not concerned with the children. The children ought to combine their labor with materials and produce toys worthy of themselves; if they depend upon the charity of others for their toys, they are bound to be disappointed." The train continued to chug down the track. Already, it had surrendered too much of its valuable time attempting to explain a truth which the true Individual grasps instinctively without explanation, and which the second-hander can never hope to understand.

"You can't abandon us!" cried the dolls.

"Yes, I can! I authorize it," said the Big Strong Engine. It chugged down the track, exuding power and authority from every gear and axle. It was a train I would be pleased to greet as an equal. I would place my hand upon its fender in a gesture of fellowship.

The train and its parasites were despondent. Then in the distance they saw another engine approaching. This engine was small. It was a female engine. Yet it moved with a quiet assurance. It would be no shame to be such a train.

"Help us!" cried the train full of parasites. "We must go over the mountain so that the children may have toys!" (A child requires no toys, of course, but a good stout twig and a bit of peeled potato, with which, and imagination, he may conjure himself any entertainment he desires. That is all I required, and I am perfect.)

"It would be difficult for me to help you," said the little engine. "I am a little engine, and this hill is quite steep."

"Please!" the toys groveled. It was sickening.

"Yet," said the little engine, "for all that, I believe I could do it."

"Oh, please!" simpered the toys. Pitiful. Disgusting.

"Yes," said the little engine, gathering steam, "I am a law unto myself, and I say that this thing is possible. I think I can, and therefore, I can. I obey my rational self-interest in so doing." The little engine hitched herself to the train of parasites and began to pull. And indeed, her force of mind was sufficient to carry her up the hill, awaiting no man's permission. "I think I can," she proclaimed, "therefore, I can."

She reached the top and surveyed the valley below with satisfaction. "I have carried you up to the top of this hill for selfish reasons," she said, "to demonstrate a point to myself. But I cannot permit your errand to be carried out." And with that, she unhitched the train full of gewgaws and parasites and watched it roll back down the mountain.

The petty gimcracks wept. Their tears, like themselves, were empty of any value. The little engine continued to chug over the hill, utterly unmoved.

Later the toys were dismantled, and their component materials were then used for practical purposes (track repairs, pewter spoons sold at a reasonable price, the putty of a plumber who understood his own worth), so it can be said that this story has a happy ending.

(To learn what became of the trains, read *Atlas Shrugged*! I state without ego that it is the best book ever written, and the truest, by any objective measure, except for *The Fountainhead*.)

---★---

Real Housewives of the Space Program, 1959

In 1959 we launched a lot of men into space because the Russians were doing so also, and that made us nervous. Those men had wives, and because it was the 1950s, they had to keep up appearances in a very stressful way. We also sent up some chimpanzees! It was a time.

BETTY GRISSOM: We are all planning matching casseroles for the space launch.

LOUISE SHEPARD: Our hairstyles also match.

TRUDY COOPER: The higher the hair, the shorter the commute to reach our husbands in the Mercury capsule!

ANNIE GLENN: And, of course, the closer to God.

TRUDY COOPER: (sipping martini) Yes, of course.

BETTY GRISSOM: We all love casserole, having big hair, and the American flag.

RENE CARPENTER: And our husbands, who are going into space.

LOUISE SHEPARD: They might explode at any moment!

ANNIE GLENN: But we're relaxed about it.

TRUDY COOPER: Yes we've all made casseroles.

MARGE SLAYTON: My casserole is heart-healthy, but not for any specific reason.

RENE CARPENTER: That's so thoughtful, Marge. Mm!

LOUISE SHEPARD: Totally unnecessary though since everyone in the space program has to have a perfect heart.

TRUDY COOPER: (to camera) Everyone knows that Deke Slayton has a cardiac anomaly, but we're too polite to say so.

RENE CARPENTER: Trudy, I can't get over how clean your place is! I almost can't believe two people have been living here in this one household together in the same city all this time!

Trudy laughs politely but her eyes are daggers.

TRUDY COOPER: Well, that's certainly what has been happening! Here in this one household in the same city, and not on the verge of divorce!

ANNIE GLENN: Would you like some pimento cheese? I have cut all the olives into the shape of tiny capsules, and the pimento is like the blast from the rocket.

LOUISE SHEPARD: (fiddling with an olive) The capsule isn't detaching properly!

Everyone laughs, first politely, then too much.

TRUDY COOPER: (to camera) We are all constantly confronted with the terrifying potential of death.

BETTY GRISSOM: (too loudly) WHO WANTS HAM LOAF?

ANNIE GLENN: I made ham loaf for Jackie Kennedy!

BETTY GRISSOM: Annie got to meet Jackie Kennedy, and she never lets us forget it.

RENE CARPENTER: If I have to hear one more time about the time Annie made ham loaf for Jackie Kennedy, I'm going to lose it.

ANNIE GLENN: There is no conflict here. We are just a group of women who love God, the space program, casserole, and having hair that defies gravity.

LOUISE SHEPARD: All of our home lives are completely regular.

TRUDY COOPER: Especially mine!

RENE CARPENTER: Especially Trudy's!

BETTY GRISSOM: We love space so much.

RENE CARPENTER: Any of our husbands could explode at any time.

Re: The Mockingbird

Harper Lee wrote To Kill a Mockingbird *and, I assume, also received mail.*

Dear Miss Lee,

Wow wow wow! So much to love here! Just one tiny note. I think the first thing a lot of people will notice (and love, as I did!) about your amazing, amazing work is the title! *To Kill a Mockingbird*. It had me right on the edge of my seat from the very beginning.

The whole time I was reading, I was like, when are they going to kill this mockingbird? That's tension. And readers love that.

But you've got to follow through on it, Miss Lee! You cannot tell your readers that you are going to kill a mockingbird and then—not only don't they kill one, but I don't believe they actually see a mockingbird at all.

I kept reading and reading and it was all very interesting, wonderful texture, with Scout and Jem and Atticus and everyone. I kept saying, this is great! But where's the mockingbird? They've got to introduce the mockingbird soon, or it won't be very satisfying when they kill it. I got to where I was getting more and more nervous every page I was turning and not finding a single mockingbird on it, and finally I went to my secretary Miss Hobbs and said, Miss Hobbs, when does the mockingbird come in, so I can skim ahead, and she said (she was filing her nails with perfect calm), oh there *isn't* a mockingbird.

That's no good. You've got to have a mockingbird in the book, Harper Lee, and they've got to kill it!

Other than that, the book is just terrific. I wouldn't change a whole lot. All you need to do is add just a little chapter, I think. Scout wakes up one morning and Jem and Atticus are putting on their hunting gear, and she says, where are you going, and they say, well, you know that mean big mockingbird who's been terrorizing the town? (You could establish this in a few sentences.) Well, we're forming a posse comitatus to go and kill it. Then Scout says she has to go with them because she hates mockingbirds and has always wanted to kill one, and they pull up where the mockingbird is. It's a big mean bird, a real bruiser, and it's strutting around thumping its chest and saying, "I'll take the whole lot of you! I'm not scared of you! I'm a mockingbird, by God, and nobody can lay a finger on me!" but Atticus just raises his gun, cool and level, and kills it with one shot.

Or when Atticus shoots the dog, he could be shooting at the dog but a mockingbird could get in the way and he could shoot it instead, if you don't like that suggestion. I think there's more than one way to kill a mockingbird, to coin an expression!

That's my only note, the mockingbird thing. I love everything else. If you have a second or third book in mind with the same characters, we'd love it! Anything with more of that hunky, uncomplicated Atticus Finch!

Cheers,
Dave

What Your Dream Means!!!

There is a long, vibrant tradition of white people confidently explaining what Dr. Martin Luther King, Jr., really meant. There must have been a first time, and I think that first time was historic in its own right. I have on good authority that that first time went something like this.

Dear Dr. King,

When I heard your speech at the March on Washington, I thought: this man needs my help! I couldn't rest until I sent you this. Whenever I see something wrong in the world, I have to make it right. That's just how I am. And when I heard your speech, it was clear to me the action I needed to take: I needed to rush to my bookcase and find my book on dream symbolism. I was in such awe as you described to a large crowd of people, in detail, a dream that you had. I have often tried to do the same (I guess people are just alike everywhere!) but I have never held a crowd the way you did. I wonder, though, if you knew the full power of what you were saying. Well, that is why I am writing. I thought you might like to know what your dream means. I have gone through all the things that you mentioned in your speech so that you can know what it is your mind was really trying to tell you with each symbol! Dreams are so fascinating! If you have any questions, please let me know.

You mention that you dream that "all men are created equal" and that you also dream about a "brotherhood of man" becoming a reality in this age. The presence of men in your dream can mean a lot! Freud believed that all men are the father: do you think this could be about your father? Men can also represent assertive, masculine energy—maybe the brotherhood of man you talk about is you embracing your masculine energies!

You mention sitting down at a table of brotherhood. Tables are where we sit when we are hungry! Did you eat enough before you went to bed and had your dream? Sometimes a dream can be the body's way of letting us know we need nourishment!

You mention skin in your dream. The skin is the largest organ in the body! Having a thin or thick skin can suggest whether you are feeling secure or vulnerable in your relationships.

You mention Alabama in your dream. Alabama doesn't appear in my dream symbolism book at all! Congratulations on finding something new to be in dreams! Same with Mississippi. Rivers can symbolize the flow of your life, but I think you meant the state.

You mention "sweltering" and "the heat of oppression" in your dream! Feeling heat in a dream can be as simple as your body letting you know that the room where you sleep is too hot. Open a window.

You mention joining hands! Hands are often symbolic of your ability to "handle" a situation. Giving yourself a "hand" is also a way to say applause. Does this help?

You mention in your dream a desire to make both mountains and hills low! They can represent obstacles. Or being "over the hill" can reflect a fear of aging. Maybe your desire for the hills and mountains to be made low is about that!

You mention children in your dream several times, both your own and those of others. Children can mean your own inner child, or they can be your subconscious's way of reminding you of an incomplete project! Is there a big project you are working on that still needs to be completed? If so, that could be what the dream is really about.

There is one thing that I can say with certainty that your dream is not about: racism!

Sincerely,
Karen

Notes on Camp, by Susan Sontag, Aged Fifteen, Camp Winnebago

These preceded her more famous Notes on Camp *by a decade and a half.*

C amp is one of those things that has been named (this one is named after the lake on which it is located) but never been described.* Indeed, when a thing is alive, it is hard to describe it (this is why no one has ever successfully described a cat, though many people have tried), but there are several reasons why Camp in particular has never been discussed: I have not been to Camp before for this length of time, and also I did not bring a notebook last year.

To snare something like Camp in words, one must be tentative and nimble. Hence, these casual notes; also diaries are liable to be stolen especially if the contents seem at all private.

1. To start very generally, Camp is a mode of being of six weeks' duration.
2. I will be attending Camp for all six weeks. I have packed everything that I was instructed to pack and am also bringing along the complete writings of André Gide, my

* Other people have probably described it but I haven't.

favorite author, not that I will have time to read them because the exigencies of Camp (application of bug spray, canoeing, group singing) will doubtless be more pressing.

3. Camp is also characterized by the presence of friends. In addition to André Gide, who will be accompanying me in spirit, my friend Emily is going to Camp this year. Emily loves Edna St. Vincent Millay and is one year my senior.

4. Characteristics of Emily:
    a. Intelligence
    b. Vitality
    c. *Douceur*
    d. A perfect small mole just above and to the left of her upper lip that moves as a kind of punctuation when she laughs

5. Camp is a period during which certain forms of affinity and certain modes of activity are to be preferred to others. Its situation may vary but tends to the rural or bucolic in preference to the urban.

6. This one is by a lake.

7. As we drive to Camp I will occupy myself by making a list of random items which are part of the canon of Camp; the car ride is quite bumpy and I apologize if they are not legible:
    a. Marshmallows
    b. Canoeing
    c. Friendship bracelets
    d. Arts and crafts
    e. Cabins
    f. Rusticism
    g. Horse girls

    h. Communal showers

    i. Postcards

    j. Letter-writing

    k. Bunk beds

    l. Talent show

    m. Warm fuzzy

    n. Cold prickly

8. We're here. More notes later.

9. Another characteristic of Camp is a bunk in a cabin. I have been assigned my bunk and have greeted Emily with due enthusiasm. We have arranged a detailed itinerary of crafts and canoeing.

10. Camp taste has an affinity for certain arts rather than others. For instance, God's Eyes, friendship bracelets, and macramé make up a large part of Camp.

11. Camp items focus less on pure decoration and more upon emotional resonance—the macramé bracelet exchanged as a token of friendship is transferred from one party to another not for its elegance but for the relationship its exchange signifies.

12. I have made Emily a friendship bracelet.

13. Another characteristic of Camp is the culmination of the weeks of Camp in a mode of performance, namely, the Camp talent show.

14. I have signed us up to perform at the Camp talent show, but Emily has demurred.

15. Some characteristic ideas for a performance at the Camp talent show, based upon my observation of the rituals of Camp

    a. Guitar (in my case this would require learning the guitar)

b.   Dance (I find that the body is ever-more exigent in its boundless exigencies, but it is a poor vessel for executing dance moves as I would like)

c.   Tell Jokes (most of my jokes depend on familiarity with works of André Gide that I doubt a Camp audience possesses)

d.   Magic (technically, sleight-of-hand, illusion; there is no magic except what is accessible through reading the works of André Gide with great attention)

e.   Skit (I have concocted many skits in my head but these demand rehearsal and performers with a shared vision)

"True friends stab you in the front."
—*Oscar Wilde, attrib.*

16.   All Camp objects and persons contain a large element of artifice.

17.   For instance, Emily states that she will wait to go to canteen *with* her friend, when her friend is ready, so that she will not be obliged to eat alone, yet departs in advance of her friend and fails to complete the simple friendly act of reserving a seat for her at table. This is a demonstration of ARTIFICE.

18.   Such a demonstration of artifice is (apparently!!!!) inherent to Camp.

19.   Another example of the artifice inherent in Camp is when one goes to sit down with one's so-called friend, and she avoids eye contact and instead stares deferentially down at her lunch, while another girl in a pink

headband (NOT on the authorized Camp packing list!) says "Actually, that seat is saved."

20. Some features of Camp include betrayal, mystery, and artifice. (For whom is such a seat saved by one's friend (one's second self) if not for one's self (one's first self)?)

21. To take another example (not to belabor the subject), supposing that Emily and her friend decided jointly and in consultation with their parents that they would attend this very Camp this summer, together, as an emblem of friendship. For Emily to conduct herself in a manner suggesting she and her friend (Susan, for want of a better name) are not even *acquainted* demonstrates a high level of artifice and indeed betrayal.

22. Emily was not at ax throwing when she explicitly vowed that she would be at ax throwing.

23. Such betrayal too is (APPARENTLY!) manifestly characteristic of Camp.

24. To reinvent the self entirely is often said to be a property of Camp in theory, but this, in practice, proves elusive.

25. Self-reinvention at Camp may be successful if undertaken spontaneously, but as a *reaction* to another deliberate act of self-creation it appears inherently suspect.

26. If Emily reinvents herself as a popular girl, Susan (for instance) may find herself stranded, and any reinvention as a lone wolf by choice who is spending a lot of time in the pottery cabin voluntarily will be inherently suspect.

27. There is nothing of interest in the pottery cabin. A characteristic of the pottery cabin is that the girls who frequent it are all losers who breathe noisily through their noses, a feat I would have considered impossible, and

wear glasses that give them the appearance of being seen through a dirty windshield. I despise the pottery cabin and I despise pottery.

28.   Clay is as fickle as friendship and as immovable as the time between the start of lunch and the finish of lunch when you are eating in the girls' bunk because you have nowhere to sit.

"Some say life is the thing but I prefer reading."
—*Logan Pearsall Smith*

29.   Books, as companions, possess none of the flaws and foibles of human beings. I have spent the better part of today in my bunk reading.

30.   I didn't really want to go to Camp anyhow (except as a cultural observer and critic; maybe I will be a cultural observer and critic when I am older). I just wanted to sit somewhere quiet and read the collected works of André Gide, and I'm just grateful to have the opportunity to do so thanks to Emily's treachery.

31.   André Gide is the only one who understands me.

32.   Every sentence that he writes is like something plucked from my own brain. I am glad I'm sitting here reading André Gide.

33.   A characteristic of Camp is that the counselors will come and ask if you are all right if you aren't at Color Wars because you have decided you would prefer to stay in your bunk and read the collected works of André Gide.

34.   I explained to the Camp counselor (blue-eyed, shocking white teeth) that it was imperative that I read the collected works of André Gide because all other pursuits

are secondary to grasping what it means to be alive and he said unprompted that I could eat lunch with the counselors if I was feeling ostracized. I explained that ostracism (from the Greek) is when one is cast out by means of a pottery shard or *ostraka* and hardly relevant here, and he said, You're all right, Sue.

35. One realization that may come to a person of (in my opinion) more than average intelligence when faced with the exiguous exigencies (one of these words is wrong) of Camp is that

36. Sorry I didn't finish that last thought my flashlight battery died.

37. Another property of Camp is the singing of asinine songs which the singer can never be said to do correctly; too little emphasis and the Camp counselors rebuke her, too much emphasis and she is made mock of by her erstwhile friends, a further manifestation of the treachery inherent in Camp.

38. Homesickness is a characteristic of Camp. To be homesick for that which one has brought with one to Camp is a paradox of Camp: to long for the very friendship which Camp ought to have secured and yet which Camp has rendered more precarious is a contradiction of the kind on which Camp thrives.

39. The writing of letters home from Camp makes manifest many of the underlying themes of Camp, yet there is a right and wrong manner of so doing. To write, "I am miserable, Emily refuses to speak to me, her new friends splashed me deliberately with their paddles when they were canoeing, and I was sitting on the end of the dock adding to my notes," would be a revelation of a kind

unsuited to Camp. Camp thrives upon the light, the airy, the reassuring. To write, "Camp is thrilling and I am making lots of new friends! I have been canoeing and on a long hike! Still, home holds its appeal," is better suited to Camp.

40. The large blotch above is just water from the aforementioned splashing; to cry would not be characteristic of Camp.

41. *The Counterfeiters* is the name of a terrific book by André Gide, but it might also be a good name for Emily and her new compatriots.

42. I ate lunch with the counselors. The counselors have their own difficulties, not un-akin to ours; they are the world in small. Much could be observed about them. Noisy sippers; given to gossip.

43. Emily stared at me all during lunch. In books (Gide does this less than others) people are always staring at one another in *manners* and understanding that the manner is forlorn or apologetic or irate, but I can't read her expression as expressions are read in books. When I looked back, she looked away.

44. After lunch as we walked back to the cabins, Emily said she was sorry and then bolted.

45. If after days of pretending ignorance of her friend's existence, Emily attempts a sally of a sort at the campfire where Susan is permitted to sit next to her and her existence acknowledged, all must be instantly forgiven and no indication of resentment at prior transgressions must be shown.

46. I don't know why this is so, but it's so.

47. The best way of cooking a marshmallow is to light it on fire; some campers maintain otherwise, but Emily and I agree.

48. Some elements of s'mores are superior to others, ranked, they are:
    a. The chocolate
    b. The marshmallow
    c. The stick
    d. The graham cracker (disgusting)

49. Some marshmallows simply must be lost to the flames; this is a characteristic of Camp.

50. Also among the aspects of Camp is the scary, or ghost story. This is told around the campfire and may induce the holding of hands at moments of heightened drama or tension.

51. The Hook-Hand Man is a terrifically terrifying story. In this narrative, a man's hand has been supplanted by a hook (Freudian?), and he travels around seeking to enact an unspecified vengeance upon the sexually liberated.

52. Emily's palms are hot but damp.

53. When the story came to the couple at the outlook "who had gone there to neck," my palm was squeezed hard in Emily's palm just a moment.

54. Is this a characteristic of Camp?

55. Reasons Emily might have squeezed my hand include:
    a. Reflex
    b. Palm itched
    c. Fear (but why at that moment?)
    d. *Tendresse*

     e.   Wanted to get my attention for reason unrelated to the story

     f.   Deliberate suggestion

56.   The pressure felt meaningful, like a Morse signal (though in Morse code it would have been E?).

57.   Possible meanings of E in Morse Code

     a.   Unclear

     b.   Emily wants to remind me of her name (unnecessary)

58.   How terribly bounded in the body one is! and yet how porous—electric—alive a thing the body is.

59.   To observe the sky at home is at once no different than doing so from Camp, and yet how different, how more numerous the stars! Orion bestrides the sky like a colossus.

"Having reached such heights of joy
that anything afterward would be a descent."
—*André Gide, The Counterfeiters*

60.   Did André Gide ever attend Camp?

61.   Camp is muddy and buggy and I dropped my marshmallow in the fire and my flashlight is out of batteries and it's terribly bad and I kissed Emily under Orion's large bright belt on the way back from the campfire and she kissed me back and it tasted like graham crackers, which I can't stand.

62.   The ultimate Camp statement: I can't stand it; it's wonderful.

63.   I can't wait to go to Camp again next year.

In Cold Blood If Truman Capote Didn't Think the Murderer Guy Was Kind of Hot

Buckley and Vidal Debate Other Things

Although their debates at the 1968 Republican and Democratic conventions are most famous, William F. Buckley, Jr., and Gore Vidal also engaged in a series of other debates of lower-profile questions; below are excerpts.

What is the best superpower?

Vidal: Immortality, no doubt, though one would sadly be no wiser at the end than when he began. Coupled with eternal youth. There is simply no better answer.

Buckley: I am not surprised to hear that Mr. Vidal has no better answer. I think it is something for which we can all be grateful that our society depends on ah higher sources of intelligence than are accessible to feline purveyors of Hollywood-minded trash who tend to expatriate themselves to Rome for a good portion of the year.

Vidal: If I expatriate myself, it is merely in search of a better vantage to contemplate Bill Buckley and his tireless efforts to precipitate the decline of the West.

Buckley: Precipitate? I don't precipitate anything, Mr. Vidal, indeed, it is you who are most vulnerable to the charge of being precipitate.

Vidal: I note you haven't offered any ideas of your own, Bill. Or were you saying that you'd like to control the weather? Or is immortality it, then?

Buckley: I feel that to promulgate a theory of immortality based upon anything other than an adherence to the teachings of Christ would not merely be presumptuous but border upon blasphemy.

Vidal: So you don't have an answer.

Buckley: Teleportation—a proposition made easier by an avoidance of the seductive doctrine of monism—

Do you prefer cats or dogs?

Vidal: Cats, naturally. One wonders that the question need be admitted.

Buckley: Dogs of course. Mr. Vidal could not possibly appreciate any beast defined by loyalty or selflessness.

Vidal: It is characteristic, I think, of you Bill and your elegant prose style to elide any appeal that a more discriminating creature might hold.

Buckley: I take it you refer to the cat as a more discriminating creature? It cannot be a much more discriminating creature if it is willing to pay court to the author of such perverted Hollywood-minded pornography as *Myra Breckinridge*.

Vidal: So you *do* read.

Should toilet paper go over the top
of the roll or under?

Buckley: This is a subject on which the author of *Myra Breckinridge* is well equipped to comment, given the most proper use to which such a text may be put.

Vidal: A tormented and convoluted image, to be sure! It is not the eschatological, then, whose immanentizing so haunts you but the scatological.

Buckley: I fear that Mr. Vidal, so busily engaged about the immanentizing of the eschaton, mistakes this remark for an instance of wit; I don't.

Would you prefer to fight a horse-sized duck
or one hundred duck-sized horses?

Buckley: One would ah hope that the escalation of the nuclear capacity in this nation has not reached such a ah febrile pitch that ducks are rendered sixteen times as large as life and more than ordinarily pugnacious.

Vidal: I must say, if I may say, Bill—I think it quite charming of you to attribute the increase in the size of the duck to some form of nuclear accident. This reveals once again the limits of your imagination.

Buckley: Not all of us are blessed with the imagination of the author of *Myra Breckinridge*, a fact for which I daily offer up hosannas on my knees.

Vidal: That such is your preferred posture will come as little surprise to avid readers of—that little magazine whose name will not pass my lips.

Buckley: Now just a minute—

Vidal: I would fight the duck.

Fear and Loathing in Las Vegas, the Draft Where Hunter S. Thompson Forgot to Bring Any Drugs

"Gonzo" journalist Hunter S. Thompson famously went to Las Vegas to cover a motorcycle event and took a lot of drugs. Well, what if he forgot to pack them? This piece explores that concept.

We were just north of Barstow when I realized I hadn't remembered to pack any drugs.

"Ah, shit," I said to my attorney. "I forgot to bring the drugs with me, and the drugs were sort of the whole premise of this thing."

"That's okay," my attorney said. "We don't need drugs to have a good time. Anyway, this is a work trip for you."

It was taking much longer to get to Las Vegas than I remembered. We were listening to the radio and driving the speed limit. We picked up a hitchhiker. The kid seemed comfortable around us. "We're on our way to Las Vegas," I explained, "to find the American Dream."

"That's nice," the hitchhiker said.

"We haven't taken any drugs," I added.

The hitchhiker's face got a concerned look, like he was trying to read something written in small print that he was holding too far away from his face for absolute comfort.

"It's a work trip," my attorney said, "for him, so it wouldn't make sense for him to take drugs."

"We're still going to have an interesting time," I told him confidently, "even though we haven't taken any drugs."

We both looked at the hitchhiker so that he would know it was his turn to speak. We expected him to say something interesting that maybe I could put in my story about the American Dream. "It's good that you haven't taken any drugs," the hitchhiker said finally. The kid looked uncomfortable.

"We don't need drugs," my attorney said. He slammed his hand on the dashboard, and the glove compartment opened to reveal some maps and the registration and a few other things it was legal for us to have in the car. "Our friendship is based on more than that."

"Our friendship is based on more than drugs," my attorney said. It was fifty miles since the hitchhiker had gotten out of the car, and we were listening to the radio and watching the desert whiz by.

A minute or two passed.

"We don't even have to talk all the time," I said.

"Yes," my attorney agreed. "That's how you know you have a real friend, when you can just be together and not even have to talk."

We drove fifty more miles, not talking.

"I'm not even mad you didn't bring the drugs," my attorney said, "because our friendship doesn't need them."

"We have plenty in common without them," I said.

"Yes!" my attorney said. He slapped the dashboard hard with the flat of his hand, and the glove compartment opened again. "Yes!"

"I might take a nap though," my attorney said.

"Go right ahead!" I said. "Nap!"

"I'm really glad we're getting to spend this time together," my attorney said.

We arrived in Las Vegas and checked into the hotel without incident. My fine motor skills were still functioning at a high level, and I had no difficulty gauging distances. When I opened my mouth, the words that came out were the words I meant to say. I made it to the elevator, but it wasn't a big deal at all that I made it to the elevator. All that it entailed was walking across the room, and I could walk across the room just fine.

"They've cleaned this place up a lot," my attorney said.

I nodded. "Many fewer bats and pterodactyls."

We got into the elevator to ride up to our room. "It's changed," my attorney said. He nodded politely at someone who had just gotten onto the elevator with us. "Better clientele."

"That's not the half of it!" I said. "The last time I was here everyone in the elevator was a lizard."

"That's what I mean," my attorney said. "I was trying to be tactful."

We sat and stared at the hotel room. It was a very normal hotel room, and nothing about it was a problem. Outside it was a neon sign that looked like a neon sign.

"I guess I'll just go cover this motorcycle event," I said.

I went to the press desk to get my press credentials.

"My name is Duke," I said. "And this is my attorney. We are here to look for the American Dream, and we are both completely sober."

"Here you go," the press credential person said. "Thanks for being here."

In the room we both drank large quantities of water to hydrate ourselves. "Hydration is very important," I said. My attorney agreed.

"We've got to be enormously hydrated to cover this motorcycle rally and find the American Dream," he said. "It could be bad if we weren't hydrated enough, because this is a desert."

I nodded. "That's a good idea," I said.

"I have a lot of good ideas," my attorney said. "We've got to be responsible! We've got to be responsible here in Las Vegas!"

I nodded in agreement. I couldn't think of anything more to say on the subject.

"I guess I'll go to the pool," I said.

My attorney took a bath without incident.

"Maybe we should see Debbie Reynolds," my attorney suggested.

"That sounds fun," I said.

I took many notes at the motorcycle rally. It was good that I took the notes, even if I did remember everything that had happened there. It's a best practice, journalistically, to take detailed notes. I was glad that I had my detailed notes and my tape recorder.

After the rally we sat at the carousel bar. It went around and around very slowly beneath the gyrating acrobatic performers who formed the main attraction of the Circus Circus, besides, of course, the gambling. My attorney ordered a rum sling. "Can I get you anything?" he asked.

"Thanks," I said, "but I shouldn't have anything. I'm driving."

We went to see Debbie Reynolds. "You don't have a ticket," the bouncers said.

"No," I agreed. "We don't. Does that mean we can't get in?"

"That's what it means," the bouncer said.

"Oh," my attorney said. "Thank you for telling us."

"You're welcome," the bouncer said.

My attorney and I walked out across the floor of the Desert Inn in a very orderly way.

"We didn't need to see Debbie Reynolds to have a good time," my attorney said. "We have our friendship."

"Maybe friendship was the real American Dream," I said.

"I like Las Vegas," I said. "It's nice here."

"It's good we didn't have the drugs," my attorney said, "because we probably couldn't have expensed them."

Richard Nixon Tapes But Just the Parts Where He's Yelling at Checkers

We know two things about President Richard Nixon. (We actually know more, but I am trying to keep this headnote short.) He had a little dog named Checkers, and he kept a lot of incriminating recordings of himself yelling at people.

Goddamn it, get in and get those files. Blow the safe and—Checkers! Checkers! No!

The way I want that handled is just to—No! What the hell is this? Checkers! What's that he's got in his mouth? Ah, hell.

Break in. Break in and take it out. Stop! Not you, Checkers. Give me that! Here, Checkers. Fetch!

I want to make sure he is a ruthless son of a bitch, do what he's told—No! Checkers! Checkers! [muffled thumping] Give me that. Give it to me. Drop it!

Ah what the hell is this—Checkers! Checkers! No! Give me that!

Goddamn it! Checkers!

I'm not for women in any job. Checkers, you were just out! You can't go out again!

The Italians, of course, those people don't have their heads screwed on right—Hey, now, buster—Pat! Pat! Checkers is in here! Get him out of here! I'm on the phone.

Got to deny everything—[sound of rolled-up newspaper striking a desk] Checkers! Down! Get down from there!

Don't shake! Ah, hell, it's everywhere—Sorry, Mr. Kissinger. . . .

I was doing a little thinking last night about this clown Harrison Williams. NO! Bad boy! Not you Mr. Hoover. Checkers has gotten into the wastebasket CHECKERS! CHECKERS STOP IT! Pat!

Aw Christ how did he get a shoe—Sorry, Mr. Kissinger.

Checkers!

Mr. Hoover. Sit! SIT! Goddamn it. Not you, Mr. Hoover. Checkers is here with me.

If on a case-by-case basis you could determine that you would want the bureau to get in, if you sort of have the scent or the smell of a national conspiracy thing, that's a different matter— BAD DOG! Checkers! Bad boy!

That's a good boy. Who's a good boy? Everybody's against Dick Nixon but you, Checkers. Oh, sorry, Secretary Deng, I didn't realize you were already on the line.

1970s
Urban Legends

Many cryptids, beings, and supernatural phenomena observed during this eventful decade have never been fully explained.

***Jonathan Livingston Seagull*:** It's on the bestseller list, and you don't know why. It's a book about a seagull who wants to live his best life, but it can't be, can it? People keep claiming to read it and enjoy it, but they can't be doing that, really, can they?

Pet Rocks: Take this into your home, they tell you. It is a rock, they say. But not just any rock. This rock will provide you companionship. You bring the rock home. But what is worse? To feel nothing at all, or actually to detect, from the rock, some form of companionship?

Mood Rings: The ring will tell you what you are feeling. The ring says that you are feeling purple. This is what purple feels like. Have you ever felt purple before? You are feeling it now. Oh no, now you are feeling puce.

Tie Dye: The fabric must first be restrained before its color can be altered. Do not forget to restrain the fabric! This one is a holdover from the 1960s.

Killer Rabbit: You are President Jimmy Carter. You are in Georgia, in a rowboat, where you think yourself safe. You are not safe. You see it coming toward you in the water, ears lowered, eyes wild with menace. It is the rare killer swamp rabbit, and it has marked you for its prey. You look around you for help, but there is no one who can save you. You are too far from shore, and the rabbit is coming. But you have your paddle. Wild with terror, you splash the ghastly apparition, and it recedes. The Washington press corps will mock you; comedians will write songs about you; all that matters is your survival. You know what you saw.

The Streaker: He is at a public event. But he is taking off all his clothes and running. Why has he removed all his clothes? To what arcane god is this a sacrifice?

Deep Throat: It lives in a parking garage. It signals its readiness to divulge by means of a flag planted in a flowerpot. It is nameless and faceless, and it is a Source. It knows about the president. People claim to have seen it and thought it was sexy, but they are talking about something different.

Bell-Bottoms: They are on all the pants now, and no one knows why. What is happening to the feet? Why are we no longer permitted to see the feet?

Disco: Art holds a mirror up to life, and disco holds a mirror ball up to life to dance under. You dance and dance, and an enormous sparkling mirrored eye hangs over your revel, watching you. It is all right. The mirror ball sees everything. The mirror ball understands.

Stagflation: You are at your 1970s job, receiving your wages. They remain constant. You go to the grocery store to buy your groceries. You pick a can of soup off the shelf, look at it, and put it back. In the time that it has taken you to pick it up, it has become twice as expensive. You go outside, and there it is in the sky, its antlers blotting everything out as it grows larger and larger—the Stagflation. It tilts back its head and bellows. The 1970s are a great time.

Nancy Reagan's Psychic's Daily Horoscopes Once She Realized They Were Being Used to Set Policy

First Lady Nancy Reagan reportedly got a lot of advice from a psychic, a thing that makes sense for FLOTUS to do and certainly doesn't worry anyone, least of all the psychic whose job it is to offer that advice.

If today is your birthday . . . You're an Aquarius, like Ronald Reagan!

Aries: This will be an exciting week for you as Mercury is in retrograde. Avoid making any long-term commitments. Someone mystic or spiritual in your life, probably a Libra, will receive surprising news about how seriously her psychic predictions are being taken by a very important person or persons, and it might send her into a bit of a spiral.

Taurus: Now is a good time to travel. Tell loved ones how you feel. Avoid impulse purchases. If you have an employee whose job it is to write horoscopes, please cut her some slack because she is trying to figure out the situation in East Germany in case the president's spouse asks if she "sees anything" about it.

Gemini: The moon is in the sign opposite yours, and cooperation is paramount. Be patient with friends and loved ones. Especially if there's a psychic in your life who doesn't know about the Laffer Curve!

Cancer: A romantic partner continues to be receptive to your influence. Consider urging him to do something about the AIDS crisis, Nancy.

Leo: This is a good week to work on a long-term project.

Virgo: Sorry! This would have been a longer, more beautiful horoscope, but I have been swamped. Do whatever you want! You're not the president.

Libra: Your stars have aligned in such a way that you will be called upon to give high-stakes advice you really do not feel qualified to give. Accept help from any source!

Scorpio: Mercury demands that you write down everything you know about Grenada and send it to the address below.

Sagittarius: Now is a good time to share knowledge with a friend, acquaintance, or psychic! Please write to the address below with information about the Laffer Curve. I am trying to find out what it is. It sounds made up.

Capricorn: A great day for romance!

Aquarius: Don't do Iran-Contra, sir.

Pisces: You will be deeply connected to your feelings. Please use them to tell me if you think a Strategic Defense Initiative would be good or bad.

※

Moon Alert: No moon alert this week! I've been too busy researching the Austrian school.

Aries: You're fine. Millions of people aren't depending on you to tell the president whether to invade places.

Taurus: According to Venus, your judgment predominates. Please write to your local psychic and tell her if the "ash heap of history" sounds cool and would be a good thing to say in a speech, or if she should keep thinking.

Gemini: Be confident in your ability to deal with a financial matter. Do you think we can outspend the Soviets on military equipment and that will work?

Cancer: A romantic partner continues to be receptive to your influence. Please do consider urging him to do something about the AIDS crisis, Nancy. A good slogan for an upcoming campaign will present itself soon.

Leo: With influence from the moon, inspiration will strike! What are good slogans for getting people to not do drugs? All I have is "Say No to Drugs," which is not a slogan, just a description of what the campaign is supposed to get people to do.

Virgo: Truly couldn't give less of shit what you do. Sorry.

Libra: You're doing okay. Don't know what else you could possibly do. Get sleep if possible.

Scorpio: Thank you for telling me about Grenada! You're the best, Scorpio!

Sagittarius: I am more confused about Laffer Curves now than I was before. Please tell me anything you know about the pros and cons of freezing the minimum wage, but in simple terms, as though I were a small child.

Capricorn: Sorry I said before that it would be a great day for romance! I was way off, and that's on me. I have had a lot on my plate lately.

Aquarius: Someone may attempt to lead you astray with curves. Don't invade Grenada unless you absolutely have to. Someone with the initials S. D. O'C. will factor prominently in your decision making.

Pisces: Be open to change, Mr. G! If you have a large wall, consider tearing it down.

50 States of Grey

Cover me with it, the economy sighed. Prosperity. I want it.

The Austrian School economist nodded enthusiastically. Here it comes, he said, do you feel it? You should be covered with it, trickling down your entire form, sliding along your Laffer Curves and your regular curves. I feel a lot of it up here.

No, the economy said, actually I don't feel anything.

Fairy Tales,
by Tom Wolfe

Tom Wolfe was a pioneer of New Journalism, which is like regular journalism but you make a big point of letting the reader know that you are Tom Wolfe writing it. Why stop at journalism, though?

So Little Red Riding Hood is walking through the woods. Why shouldn't she! It's a free country! It's the freest, greatest country in the world! Why shouldn't she shoulder a basket full of baked goods, hard rolls, pretzels, bread loaves, crescent rolls, bagels, breadsticks, and cookies and head straight into the woods, straight for Grandmother's house? That's what everyone is rushing around for, the woodsmen in their little wooden shacks, the pigs, the serving wenches, even the birds, each in their own way: to get into those woods, the woods where everything happens. To get to the woods and grab all the goodies that are there for the taking, fistfuls of gingerbread and breadcrumb trails leading who knows where, and ladders and ladders worth of golden hair, leading up, up, up! Why not go to those woods and get some of what's on offer?

So Little Red Riding Hood is on the path. She's remembering her mother's admonition: Keep to the path, Little Red! Don't stray from that path!

But she can't help thinking, just for a split second: suppose she strays from the path? Suppose she takes a step, or two, off the path altogether, deeper into those woods? The flowers are better there. Why not? Why not stray, if you're in the woods?

🔥

Unbelievable! He can't believe it! He can't believe what he's seeing in his house! This girl, this little golden-haired girl, this Jenny-come-lately, four feet nothing of flounces and bows, she's sitting *in his house*. Not only his house, *in his chair! His sanctum sanctorum! His private citadel of solitude, where his family sleeps! His family!* And not only that—in front of her—a bowl— half empty—she's eating his *goddamned porridge! Unthinkable!* He can't believe the evidence of his senses. His whole body is a live wire. His heart is going at a crazy rate. This little girl has come into his house and eaten his porridge. Just like that! As if it's her place! As if a girl can simply walk into a house, not her house even, and eat the porridge there! He'd be within his rights to eat her, you bet your grizzly ass! All the other bears would back him up.

🔥

Greed! That was the four-letter five-letter word, the unspoken, understood thing that was motivating these—pigs! These— swine! The wolf couldn't believe his eyes. They were sitting there in their little houses, their little houses of straw and sticks, try- ing to one-up each other. One-up another pig, who has a straw house, with your stick house! It was beyond words. He wanted to laugh aloud.

But he didn't laugh. Instead, he blew. Piff! Up went the straw house, like it was nothing! Which is all it was! A bunch of straw. This pig had the audacity to think that it was safe in its house of straw. This pig was, to put it bluntly, a moron. Up went the straw house and up went the stick house, right after it! Eugh. He didn't even want to eat the pigs after that. The one pig he actually respected was in the brick house, and that pig was too secure to get at. Never mind! He'd go down the chimney. Suppose he got a little singed. Well, so what? That was life.

🔥

Hansel and Gretel were looking at each other, and you could see on their faces, *This is it!* The brass ring! This was something to write home about! A gingerbread house, with all the trappings. Glazed sugar windows and the works! And nobody guarding it! My God, how lucky could two kids be? They start stuffing their pockets with the stuff, filling their chipmunk cheeks with it, great gobbets of gingerbread, thick plates of icing, almond drops, gumdrops, powdered sugar, candy canes! They're going to get while the getting is good! They're going to get their piece of the pie. And why shouldn't they? It's the 1980s!

The Team at Build-a-Bear Responds on the Thirteenth Anniversary of 9/11

Gentlemen! As you know, tomorrow is 9/11. And you know what that means: we've got to do a tweet!

We've *got* to?

The silence of Build-a-Bear on the thirteenth anniversary of 9/11 would speak volumes. Our thousands of followers are not going to want this date to pass unremarked.

I mean, it is 9/11. I don't think it's going to pass unremarked.

They are going to look to Build-a-Bear for content as they do every day, and there won't be any content.

With respect, I think you are laboring under a large misapprehension about how people view the Build-a-Bear Twitter account.

Build-a-Bear cannot be silent! When they think about 9/11, they must not forget Build-a-Bear.

Must . . . must they not?

But it must be tasteful. Greg, are you writing this down?

I have written down "9/11 tweet that helps people remember Build-a-Bear but tasteful."

Okay, ideas please.

"We Will Never Forget"

Great! But I need more!

"We Will Never Forget" and a flag.

Yes! I love this! More!

I think that's fine.

Oh, Greg. Greg. Where's the bear of it all? This feels so generic. It could come from anyone. Nothing about it says Build-a-Bear.

Honestly I think that is just fine, given that it is a 9/11 anniversary tweet.

I think it needs a bear.

Do we? We don't want to be the commemorative Pearl Harbor SpaghettiO.

The mistake that SpaghettiOs made with their Pearl Harbor tweet was simple, Greg. The Pearl Harbor SpaghettiO was smiling gormlessly. Smiling! On the anniversary of Pearl Harbor! We would never make such a mistake. Our 9/11 Build-a-Bear would be respectful. Saluting perhaps. Or standing at attention with its little paws folded. Maybe a camouflage bear with little bear dog tags, in boots. Standing next to a flag. And the flag says "We Will Never Forget," and then underneath it'll say "Build a Bear Workshop" in a cheerful font. Greg, you just made a sound.

No sound, sir.

It will be perfect! People will never forget it!

Again, not a characteristic I think people generally want a brand's tweet on the 9/11 anniversary to possess.

Just watch, Greg. I'm tweeting it now.

The tweet existed a mere fifteen minutes before being deleted.

Ragnarok in the Hall of Presidents

It is Ragnarok in the Hall of Presidents. The sun sinks below the rim of the sea for the last time; the Epcot Center collapses in on itself; the animatronic presidents twitch to life for their final battle.

★

George Washington rises from his seat and begins pulling out all his false teeth, one by one. As he hurls each tooth, he shouts the story of its origins, if it was carved from hippopotamus bone or wrenched from a living mouth, and with each tooth that lands, a soldier rises up until there is an army of them, ready to fall upon the presidents in the hall. The last tooth he pulls out is his real one.

★

John Adams cowers behind his chair as the army rises from Washington's teeth; to him, this is all a nightmare. "I am sorry for the Alien and Sedition Acts!" he cries, but no one is listening.

★

Thomas Jefferson finally lets go of the wolf he has been holding by the ears, and the wolf devours him, and as the wolf does so, Thomas laughs, the relieved laugh of a man who has always known that he merited punishment but refused to alter his course. James Madison tries to crouch behind the shelter of his political writings, but the factious hands of the unseen multitude reach out of the floor and tear him apart.

★

Monroe and John Quincy Adams square up to fight the newly risen tooth army but the army's attention is distracted by Andrew Jackson, who screams and screams as the bullets that he has carried inside his body his whole life continue on their halted trajectory toward his heart, moving inch by agonizing inch through all his internal organs. A pit has opened before him, and John Quincy Adams falls into it with a low cry; a tentacle reaches from the pit. Andrew Jackson nods with recognition, even as his body spasms in agony; it is the National Bank, in its most monstrous form. The National Bank will have its vengeance. It catches Andrew Jackson and twines its longest tentacle about his body, and then Old Hickory vanishes below; there is silence, followed by a scream.

★

Martin Van Buren is there too. He mutters excitedly in Dutch, but no one understands or hears him. William Henry Harrison's nemesis, a light rain, is now falling, and he shudders and succumbs with a groan. John Tyler looks around for allies, but he is John Tyler and no one is standing with him. Where is James K. Polk? He slinks toward the border with Mexico but is pulled abruptly back. Once was enough. Zachary Taylor's nemesis, a bowl of dangerously raw cherries, is rolling around the stage in hot pursuit of the general; he skips out of its way and gets sucked into the path of a tooth-soldier. Millard Fillmore is slowly transforming into a duck; he shrugs; such is life.

★

Franklin Pierce is too depressed to deal with any of this. He lowers his head between his knees and listens. Faintly, in the distance, he hears a low mournful whistle. The train is coming again. He has waited so long for the train. His face is streaked with tears.

★

James Buchanan sinks into a welter of indecision and is swallowed by lava. This is no less than he deserves.

★

Abraham Lincoln fights manfully against the tooth phalanx, wielding his chair with firm, strong strokes. But then he hears smug, mocking applause from the back row. There is another animatronic figure there, and he is armed. It is John Wilkes Booth; perfectly articulated and life-size. He pulls out his pistol and fires.

★

Andrew Johnson covers his ears and makes himself as small as he can. He creeps over to Ulysses S. Grant, but Grant is too busy trying to surround himself with good, trustworthy men and failing. He is not to blame, but the people he has surrounded himself with are. Rutherford B. Hayes and Chester A. Arthur are consumed by their whiskers; James Garfield is shot once and lives, but then his true enemies, the doctors, appear. They get him.

★

Benjamin Harrison looks around for help, but he is surrounded by Clevelands. They press steadily closer, crushing him. He whistles to his pet opossums, Mr. Reciprocity and Mr. Protection, but they cannot help him. There will be no reciprocity today. There will be no protection.

★

Andrew Johnson has almost made it to the door, carefully skirting the edge of the lava, when James Buchanan's arm extends from the burbling fire and pulls him into the pit. He clutches for balance and pulls McKinley with him. As McKinley goes, the pit belches with satisfaction. It remembers what he did in the Philippines.

★

But there is Teddy Roosevelt, primed for battle. He joins forces with Grant, and they fight back to back. Teddy exults in every minute of it, exerting himself too much, but he brings needed spirit to the endeavor. Taft tries to join him, but TR spurns Taft's aid and mutters something about big business. Taft sighs. He wishes he were in the hall of Supreme Court Justices. But he is in the Hall of Presidents, where there is no justice, only reckoning.

★

Woodrow Wilson's glasses have fogged up, and he cannot see. The fog on his lenses becomes thicker and thicker until it takes on a light and color of its own; a film is projected out of his eyes. The film is by D. W. Griffith. Light begins to spew from Wilson's mouth and eyes; he splits open like a hideous larva, and Edith Wilson springs out of him, glances around her with suspicious eyes, and then falls forward, impaled by Teddy Roosevelt's blade. Roosevelt has gotten a blade somehow. He is out of control, and the madness of battle is upon him. He bares his teeth and bellows.

★

Warren G. Harding is swallowed by a thick cloud of cigar smoke. He tries to signal a halt. He gestures to indicate that he is pulling some important papers out of his pocket. The papers will make everything clear! But the papers are nothing but letters he has written in which he refers to his penis as "Jerry." At this revelation, Warren begins to melt from sheer embarrassment. The tooth-soldiers turn away in disgust. They look for Calvin Coolidge. But he is nowhere to be found. They listen for him, but there is only silence.

★

Herbert Hoover backs away from the carnage seeking a corner just around which good times will be, but there are no corners to be found. The wall is curved and smooth; he inches back along it until a great swirling cloud of dust swallows him.

★

Franklin Delano Roosevelt reaches for his cigar lighter but cannot find it. He realizes that he is not sitting at his desk at all. He is engaged in a game of poker with a number of other Democratic presidents, and for some reason his head is thrown back in laughter. He blinks but the vision does not dissipate.

★

FDR has at his command great armies of men to do works and make progress, and he tells some of them to dig holes and others to fill them. But they are filling the holes too fast. He must think of another task for them, and quickly! There is a glint of hunger in their eyes.

★

Harry Truman is radioactive now, but not the exciting kind of radioactive where he gains the powers of a spider; the other kind. The bad kind. Dwight Eisenhower is managing to fight off the tooth-soldiers despite Richard Nixon clinging to his ankles. John F. Kennedy turns his head to follow the commotion and his hand catches on something strange and leathery and as big as a man; he turns to see what it is and his face falls. It is Jerry. There is no Warren G. Harding any longer, only Jerry. He tries to pull his hand free, but it is stuck.

★

Then he hears a battle yell. Straitlaced Vermont Presbyterian Calvin Coolidge flings himself at Harding's hideous priapic monstrosity. The two of them vanish into the pit, wrestling to eternity. And all without Cal uttering a word. Behind Kennedy, Johnson begins to sweat. It always pains him to see something bad happen to a Johnson.

★

Nixon is sweating so profusely that a small lake has formed beneath him. He begins to drown, but he will not release Eisenhower's ankle, and Eisenhower goes under too.

★

Jerry Ford tackles it to try to stop it, but the tackle doesn't work; oh well. Animatronic Jimmy Carter remains seated, watching all this unfold. He is at peace with himself. But Reagan is up and trying to rally his forces. As he opens his mouth to speak, he suddenly starts to recall. He recalls everything. He clutches his head in horror.

★

George H. W. Bush grabs a nearby telephone. There must be someone at the CIA who can assist him. It rings and rings and there is no answer. Lacking defenses, Clinton seizes his saxophone. He blows three final, mournful blasts, and the walls of the Hall of Presidents shake and start to crumble.

★

George W. Bush reaches into his jacket for a weapon, but there are no weapons where he thought there would be weapons. There is only a copy of *The Pet Goat*. He pulls it out and starts reading it, but it does not hold his attention. Not as the walls cave in.

★

President Obama looks at the melee and the shaking walls. He nods once to himself and walks over to where President Trump is standing. "Given the circumstances," he says, "I believe I can say something to you that I have been repressing for a long time. Frankly, Donald, I don't think that you have been very good for the country." He nods once, with finality, and walks back to his seat. In the distance he can hear a faint droning whirr, now growing louder. It will arrive soon enough.

★

President Trump is just happy to be in Florida.

★

The droning grows louder, but in Joe Biden's wax ears, it is no drone at all. It is a great puffing and chugging and whistling of steam. A train! A Scranton train! It is coming at last. "Take me!" Joe Biden cries to his metal steed. "Take me to Delaware!" But that is not exactly where the train is going.

POP QUIZ!

When this book was first published, I traveled to many places and talked to many people about fake US history. But I realized something was missing. If you have voluntarily obtained a copy of a fake textbook, you are the sort of person who will be delighted at the prospect of a surprise quiz. So here is one now! Let's see if you were paying attention in class.

1) According to Parson Weems's George Washington biography, *The Life of Washington*, which of the following did George Washington's father say to him when he said that he could not tell a lie—he had cut down the cherry tree?

   A) "Thank you for your honesty" or
   B) "Run to my arms, you dearest boy, run to my arms; glad am I, George, that you killed my tree; for you have paid me for it a thousand fold. Such an act of heroism in my son is more worth than a thousand trees, though blossomed with silver, and their fruits of purest gold"?

(It's B—wild, given that the whole point of this anecdote is the importance of not making up lies!)

2) "Liberty's mouth was so close to my face that his whiskers tickled my ear. I whispered back, 'Nobody is going to use you. They might as well try to tame a thousand wild horses with nothing but a whistle.'" Is this or is this not a line from Rush Limbaugh's series of self-insert historical fiction novels for middle-grade readers?

(IT IS! The series is called the Adventures of Rush Revere, and this line is from *Rush Revere and the Brave Pilgrims*.)

3) What Is Coming If John Quincy Not Be Coming: According to the campaign song, "Little Know Ye Who is Coming, If John Quincy Not Be Coming," what is coming if John Quincy Adams not be coming?

   A) Famine
   B) Bannin'
   C) Plunder
   D) Wonder
   E) Slavery
   F) Knavery
   G) Jobbin'
   H) Robbing
   I) Knives
   J) Fear and Pestilence
   K) Hatin'
   L) Satan
   M) All of the above

(It's M.)

4) Which of the following were real pets owned by Teddy
    Roosevelt?

A) Jonathan Edwards, a bear
B) Eli Yale, a macaw
C) Dr. Johnson, a guinea pig
D) Admiral Dewey, a guinea pig
E) Fighting Bob Evans, a guinea pig
F) Bill, a lizard
G) At least three snakes
H) Two more guinea pigs with less exciting names
I) Maude, a pig
J) A hyena, also named Bill
K) Tom Quartz, a kitten
L) General Grant, a pony
M) Baron Spreckle, a hen
N) A one-legged rooster
O) Several animals I am not even mentioning, including
    multiple rabbits and dogs

(All of the above. Everything about him makes more sense when
you know this. "Speak softly and carry a big stick"? Yes. There is
a hyena in your house.)

5) Is the following true of Cat Garfield or President Garfield?

- Was born in the kitchen of Mamma Leoni's Italian
  Restaurant?
  o CAT GARFIELD

- Was fed beef broth rectally for three months until he died?
  - PRESIDENT GARFIELD

- Loves lasagna?
  - CAT GARFIELD

- Would have preferred lasagna to being fed beef broth rectally for three months and then dying, which happened to him?
  - PRESIDENT GARFIELD

- Mike Pence delivered a birthday address to him on the floor of the House of Representatives?
  - CAT GARFIELD

- Mike Pence described him as "a human in a cat suit" and "a large orange American tradition."
  - CAT GARFIELD

- Hates Mondays
  - CAT GARFIELD

- Hates Mondays, the day he died in 1881 after being shot by Charles Guiteau and then being fed beef broth rectally for three months?
  - PRESIDENT GARFIELD

- Is alone in an abandoned house and has hallucinated every interaction we associate with him for the past forty-plus years, according to one Halloween strip in the 1980s?

   o CAT GARFIELD

Acknowledgments

They say the best way to learn facts about things is to publish something slightly incorrect, so I am excited to learn lots of new facts! I did my best, though!

1. I am sorry, I know Checkers was dead!
2. I am sorry; that first Cotton Mather example actually happened in England with a family called the Durents and he was using it as a precedent!
3. I am sorry, I know that's not how long it takes a letter to cross the Atlantic!

Tom! My goodness. Thank you for being unbelievably encouraging and unbelievably patient and dragging this book kicking and screaming into the world despite every possible chaotic life event that could have occurred, including the arrival of an actual infant kicking and screaming into the world. I appreciate you so much.

Anna, you are a wonderful agent, human, and friend, and I could not have done any of this without your exuberance, sagacity, appreciation for Grover Cleveland jokes, and boundless patience. Katrina, thank you for being magnificent and encouraging and helping to keep all my chaotic trains running smoothly and on time.

Huge thanks to Hilary McClellan, fact-checker extraordinaire, for the use of your keen brain and keen eyes (RIP Checkers). Thanks to Ursula Miller for her illustration of Walden Pond.

With much love and appreciation to my parents for instilling in me a lifelong love of history, especially U.S. history, and for many summers spent tramping around battlefields and through historic homes and farms and on every sort of nerdy adventure. I was taking it in, as it turns out.

Steve, I will probably never win at roulette because I used up so much of my lifetime share of luck getting you as a spouse. This book, like most of my endeavors, would have been impossible without you. And thanks to my wonderful in-laws, both for generating Steve and for being swell yourselves.

Also grateful for the Food Brigade, for my cherished trivia friends, JGolds, Baked & Wired (RIP quiche), my wonderful colleagues, my editor Drew, and Fred, without whom nothing.